AMA
BUSINESS
BOOT
CAMP

AMA
BUSINESS
BOOT
CAMP

Management and Leadership
Fundamentals That Will See You
Successfully Through Your Career

EDITED BY
EDWARD T. REILLY

AMACOM
American Management Association
New York · Atlanta · Brussels · Chicago · Mexico City · San Francisco
Shanghai · Tokyo · Toronto · Washington, D. C.

Bulk discounts available. For details visit:
www.amacombooks.org/go/specialsales
Or contact special sales:
Phone: 800-250-5308
Email: specialsls@amanet.org
View all the AMACOM titles at: www.amacombooks.org
American Management Association: www.amanet.org

This publication is designed to provide accurate and authoritative information in regard to the subject matter covered. It is sold with the understanding that the publisher is not engaged in rendering legal, accounting, or other professional service. If legal advice or other expert assistance is required, the services of a competent professional person should be sought.

LIBRARY OF CONGRESS CATALOGING-IN-PUBLICATION DATA
Reilly, Edward T.   AMA business boot camp : management and leadership fundamentals that will see you successfully through your career / Edward T. Reilly.
      p. cm.   Includes index.   ISBN 978-0-8144-2001-0   1. Executive ability.
2. Management. 3. Leadership. I. American Management Association.
II. Title. III. Title: Business boot camp.
   HD38.2.R45 2013   658—dc23   2012024967

ABOUT AMA
American Management Association (www.amanet.org) is a world leader in talent development, advancing the skills of individuals to drive business success. Our mission is to support the goals of individuals and organizations through a complete range of products and services, including classroom and virtual seminars, webcasts, webinars, podcasts, conferences, corporate and government solutions, business books, and research. AMA's approach to improving performance combines experiential learning—learning through doing—with opportunities for ongoing professional growth at every step of one's career journey.

Printing number

10 9 8 7 6 5 4 3 2 1

Contents

Contents

Contents

For more help with the management issues raised in
AMA Business Boot Camp please go to:
www.amacom.org/go/AMABusiness

Acknowledgments

The American Management Association is a natural meeting place for leaders and managers looking for solutions. The knowledge gathered here has many sources, and I would like to thank our developers, the staff and faculty who over the years pulled the content together into incredibly powerful courses, and the participants who make our experiential learning courses unique. It's their contributions that make our courses increasingly effective learning experiences and the content of this book so insightful.

I would also like to thank those involved with the production of the book, including the writer, Maryann Karinch, who carefully worked her way through a number of AMA programs and distilled their essence in this book, and my editor, Christina Parisi, who helped with the selection of the content and the overall direction of the text. Christina has been an outstanding editor at AMACOM for many years and proved with this project that she has remarkable diplomacy and tact as well. I also want to thank Andy Ambraziejus, the managing editor, who gets things done on time and with flawless execution. I now know firsthand why he is such a favorite with our long list of talented authors. And I would also like to thank the copyeditor, Karen Brogno, who has been improving the grammar, spelling and punctuation of AMACOM books for years.

Management and business are as much art as they are science. Our efficacy as leaders and managers is influenced by the people and experiences we have encountered along the way. I'd like to thank a few of the people who have helped define my personal leadership over the years. Dr. Eugene McCoy, who was for many years the head of the management department at St. Francis College and who taught me the value of teaching management skills in context. Don Fruehling, my boss in one capacity or another for most of my career at McGraw-Hill. He gave me the opportunity to grow and experience a broad range of business functions. The late Ted Ammon, founder and chairman of Big Flower Press, who taught me the value of risk tolerance and the importance of the capital formation structure in the United States and how essential it is to the growth of our economy.

During my years at AMA, I have benefited from a dedicated and talented Board of Trustees. They in turn have been led by the remarkable chairs Bill Slate, Terry McCaslin and Charlie Craig, who have been so supportive of me, the AMA staff, and our faculty. And they have always remained closely focused on AMA's mission.

For the past fifteen years, my executive assistant, Barbara Cashin, has proved over and over the importance of having at least one member of a team who possesses excellent organizational skills.

Finally my wife and partner in my career, Sue, who has managed the development of our family with world-class results and on many occasions helped me see through business problems with uncommon clarity.

Preface

For the past ninety years, the American Management Association has been devoted to the development of managers and leaders throughout their careers. During that time, literally millions of managers and leaders around the world have benefited from AMA's carefully developed seminars, workshops, and books produced by the outstanding faculty and authors who come together to form the backbone of AMA's ability to help people grow in their professional skills.

AMA currently teaches over 160 different seminar topics, covering much of the management landscape. We provide hundreds of webinars, webcasts, podcasts, newsletters, and of course books, which add to the richness of the information available to help managers develop their skills and become more effective. We customize hundreds of individual programs for companies around the world, which ties our insight, experience, and content directly to their business circumstances and helps the entire enterprise move toward a more efficient, effective performance.

This is an important time in the evolution of the business community in the U. S. and around the world. Economic challenges brought about by the financial collapse in 2008 have caused a great deal of disruption that will have a lasting effect for many years to come.

Now, more than ever, we need to relearn and revisit the basics and finetune our skills. We face circumstances that require virtually flawless execution, and we hope you will look to AMA and all of its resources as the perfect place to help you revitalize your own skills and those of your organization.

It is my hope that this book will be an introduction to the principles of effective, efficient management and leadership for some of the people we don't yet touch and that the collective skills they begin to develop through the exposure to these ideas will help them and their organizations. It is our intention to help people become more effective in contributing to the economic engine, which is so essential to our society, prosperity, and security.

For many people, this may be their first exposure to the principles included in this book. For others, it will serve as a comprehensive checklist of the many tasks we must master and execute in the process of becoming successful managers and leaders.

In any case, I hope people will refer back to these pages frequently, as it has been my experience that we all need to be consciously mindful of the many principles of leading and managing people and processes we use on a daily basis in order to be effective. To paraphrase Peter Drucker, management is neither an art nor a science, but rather a practice.

As with all of our work at AMA, it is my hope that this book will be a helpful tool in the development and refinement of your career.

Edward T. Reilly
President and CEO
American Management Association

A Guide to Using This Book

tions. Many of the decisions regarding who you surround yourself with are among the most important you will make.

Chapter 3: Managing Staff Changes

Need help getting things done or replacing an employee? This chapter teaches the basics of recruiting, interviewing, and selecting employees.

Chapter 4: Managing Projects

If you are dealing with a new project this chapter will walk you through setting up the project scope, putting together a team, establishing the project flow, creating a plan, and executing the project.

The pace of change has increased dramatically in recent years, reflecting among other thing the effect of global competition and the rapidly changing pace of technological development. Many times this change requires the successful handling of a project that is outside the routine activity of the business unit. How effectively you handle these "outside" projects will likely affect the perception of your success as a manager.

Section II: Senior Management Skills

Chapter 5: Strategic Thinking

Moving from management into leadership requires a shift in your skills. Most organizations need a strategy, a longer term vision of what needs to be done. They also need a series of tactics, those things that will be done in the shorter term that will advance the organization's goals envisioned in the strategy. You will want to be prepared to think strategically and act tactically.

This chapter will review the classic strategic thinking model, SWOT analysis, developing a vision and strategic frame of reference, and how to balance making the vision a reality along with successful management of day-to-day operations.

Chapter 6: Leadership

Starting with a self-assessment, this chapter will help you transition into thinking like a leader. It includes determining and developing your leadership style, building power and influence, dealing with office politics, and motivating and leading "difficult" people.

So much of the success of an organization is dependent on the ability of its staff to lead as well as manage. You will want to revisit this chapter many times and use it as a springboard for additional reading and work on developing your leadership skills.

ESSENTIAL MANAGEMENT SKILLS

Learning business "in the trenches" counts for a great deal, but taking time out to buff up your business skills enables you to telescope: to shift perspective and see the corporate landscape. Your enhanced view of what capabilities the organization needs and what capabilities it already has provides tremendous value, particularly when combined with management skills.

CHAPTER 1

Basic Management

On a day-to-day basis, managers need to know the answers to the "how much" and "where" questions: How much time, money, and staffing are required for a project? Should the top talent and big dollars go to project A or project B?

Regardless of your talent for handling numbers or precision in judging how long a task takes, your success as a manager hinges on your interaction with people.

THE ROLES OF MANAGER

The core responsibility of a manager is getting work done through others. To step into a workplace and make a difference, you need to act on the premise that, as a manager, you are no longer responsible for what you alone accomplish. You no longer hold the identity of an individual contributor and therefore your success is no longer measured by the completion of your work alone. As a manager, you now must interact with your direct reports and coordinate their efforts to achieve your departmental and your organizational goals.

Your capacity to identify the needs of your people and to apply and cultivate their abilities underlies your ability to achieve results through them. You have to play many roles as you take these actions; how well you do that will directly determine your effectiveness as a manager.

The eight primary roles that belong in your repertoire as manager are these:

1. *Leader.* Leaders adopt a big-picture view and consider day-to-day requirements in terms of mission and goals. They determine where the organization needs to go and then move forward by thinking strategically about the directions they need to take. They need to have persuasive abilities to help the organization realize their vision. They also form relationships beyond the organization and maintain its reputation.

2. *Director.* Directors define a problem and take the initiative to determine a solution. Using planning and goal-setting skills, the director determines what to delegate and ensures that other individuals understand their scope of work, specific tasks, and challenges.

3. *Contributor.* Contributors focus on tasks and work, ensuring they are personally productive, in addition to motivating others to ensure the organization's productivity hits its highest potential.

4. *Coach.* Coaches develop people through a caring, empathetic orientation that includes being supportive, considerate, sensitive, approachable, open, and fair.

5. *Facilitator.* Facilitators foster a collective effort for the organization, building cohesion and teamwork and managing interpersonal conflict.

6. *Observer.* Observers stay attentive to actions and relationships around them, determining whether people are meeting their objectives and watching to see that the unit meets its goals. Observers also have responsibility for understanding what is

important for the team to know and averting information over-load.

7. *Innovator.* Innovators facilitate adaptation and change, paying attention to the changing environment, identifying trends impacting the organization, and then determining changes needed for the organization's success.

8. *Organizer.* Organizers take responsibility for planning work, as well as organizing tasks and structures. They then follow up to ensure tasks are completed by attending to technological needs, staff coordination, and crisis handling.

Search for the keywords and key concepts in the eight role descriptions to get a clear sense of what skills you must have to function well as a manager: *plan, delegate, motivate, support, team-build, inform, change, coordinate.* All of these functions are covered in the upcoming pages.

Consider first, however, that the foundation for playing all your roles well and exercising the spectrum of management skills is a healthy work environment.

Take a look at how this spectrum of roles (identified in parentheses) plays out in a real work environment, namely, within the division of a major technology company serving the federal government market.

Michael V. Martucci held the position of marketing director for the Washington, D.C., operation of a major multinational computer company. He knew that a strong alliance with the primary value-added reseller (VAR) selling his company's products to the federal government was essential to success (Leader). He further determined that a problem existed because the VAR alone did not have the resources to showcase the products properly, so the division needed to stage a major product-related event in collaboration with the VAR (Director). He reached out to his direct reports in marketing, his colleagues in media relations, and the sales and engineering teams to alert them that a new push in collaboration with the VAR was necessary to ensure success in the market (Contributor). The most junior members of the marketing team had doubts about their ability to contribute to such a significant effort, so he pinpointed areas where their talents specifically matched project requirements (Coach). He brought everyone together and painted a picture of what needed to be done. He also admitted that he needed them to share their insights about how to stage this big event in collaboration with the VAR because, frankly, it hadn't been done before (Facilitator). He gave them a vision and a working plan, turned them loose to flesh out the plan and develop a program of action, and then had each group come back to him with their progress reports (Observer). His next move was to introduce each group's plan to the other groups, along with a proposal to coordinate the efforts and approaches. Each group had to change its plan a little, but they all had the same goal, so people handled the modifications well once the vision was clear (Innovator). Mike's other major contribution was to provide everyone with a map of how the event would flow—from preparation through execution—and to make sure that event coordinators had checklists not only to stage the event, but also to handle any crisis (Organizer). The event with the VAR brought both participation and accolades from the CEO and excellent media coverage for the company. Sales followed.

CREATING THE RIGHT ENVIRONMENT

In days gone by, an organization chart conveyed hierarchy more than interrelationships and "manager" meant "boss." Managers and their peers operated in a directive style, telling people what to do and then closely supervising them as they carried out the directive. The opposite structure is a flat organization—that is, departments or even entire companies in which levels of authority have little significance and every person is effectively his own boss. The idea is that competent workers have more motivation to be productive when they participate in the decision-making process, rather than focus on what the supervisor says and how to please that person. Over time, the shift toward flat has changed the demands on managers and the expectations that workers have in dealing with them.

The Nature of Decision Making

The "telling what to do" model for decision making has a place in organizations, but creates an uneasy environment when it becomes the default. Effective managers know when, and how, to ask for input on a decision, listen to majority opinion, forge consensus when necessary, and delegate.

Peter Earnest (*Business Confidential*, AMACOM) became executive director of the International Spy Museum after twenty-five years as a clandestine officer for the Central Intelligence Agency and another eleven years in senior executive roles at CIA headquarters. When it comes to making decisions about exhibits and "spy adventures" at the museum, Peter must adopt an I-say-you-do approach. The alternative is to risk having the creative minds on the education-program team come up with something that's more Hollywood than it is grounded in reality. By using that directive approach when necessary but only when necessary he gives the team clarity on when and to what extent they can innovate and make decisions independently.

Characteristics of a Healthy Workplace

The environment that engenders a healthy working relationship has several key characteristics, namely:

- ➤ People working together have clear expectations for the work to be completed. The direct reports and their managers share a vision of the tasks at hand.

- ➤ The team has the knowledge, skill, and motivation to get the job done. Managers pay attention to their direct reports' behavior to make that determination.

→ Each individual's needs and drivers merit consideration by the managers.

→ Individuals receive coaching for improved performance.

→ Peers and teams have effective ways of working together that enable them to collaborate on projects.

When you create the right environment, achieving results through others becomes much easier. Your aim is to help create the right motivational situation to ensure your department's success.

Misaligned relationships with former peers and confused expectations with managers above you are common obstacles to creating that kind of environment.

One of the most difficult aspects of being a new manager is supervising people who were formerly your peers and may now resent the power shift. Be objective, fair, and focused on making the most of your new career opportunity and confirming your senior manager's opinion that you were indeed the best candidate for the job.

Another perspective on the power shift involves your senior manager seeing you in the new role. Establish expectations with that person so that you aren't dealing with the vestiges of your previous job or your predecessor's job performance.

To prevent these obstacles from taking shape, or to tear them down once they have started to form, you need strong communication skills. These skills are also fundamental to your success in the roles you play as a manager.

EFFECTIVE COMMUNICATION: HONING THE KEY SKILL

New managers commonly make the mistake of focusing almost exclusively on upward communication. They worry about what their "boss" thinks of them, believing that the boss is the most important person to please. They give little thought to the people who really control their future: their direct reports.

Your employees will have more influence on your success than any other group or individual. Their ability to function and add value to the organization depends on your ability to communicate effectively with them, which is as important as your efforts to connect, in speech and writing, up the chain of command.

The Content of Business Communication

Regardless of whom you're communicating with, the first step in improving communication is to recognize *what* you need to communicate. Consider these categories of important information as a starting point for organizing your thoughts on communicating upward:

→ Performance reports

→ Situation reports

→ Recommendations

→ Requests for additional resources

→ Planning

Each of these items is either self-explanatory or examples will come later in this section. One type of communication that bears a closer look here is the situation report, called a SITREP by military personnel. Updating those higher up the chain of command about changes in the status of your project or program reduces the possibility of their making decisions based on old or tainted information. A situation report does not have to be long; in fact, it's better if the communication stays succinct.

In the battlefield, it might take shape as a ten-second call to a senior officer. For example: "On the Blue Route at RP 9. Enemy sighted at RP

7. No weapons fired. On schedule to reach tarmac by 1800. Radio silence until then."

In the office, it might be a two-sentence e-mail to the boss: "Customer complaint over system performance addressed in on-site call today. Final test of system upgrades 9 a.m. Thursday."

Similarly, when communicating to your direct reports, consider these categories of information as a starting point for organizing your thoughts:

→ Procedures

→ Project information

→ Scheduled meetings

→ Conference calls

→ Team objectives and goals

→ Employee performance

→ Key personnel shifts

→ Change in major customer/stakeholder relationship

→ Good/bad financial news

Each of these communication types receives more individual attention in subsequent chapters on performance and project management.

Communication Process

The communication process involves certain components, and your awareness of them will help keep you on track in terms of what you express and how you express it.

The sender develops a message that is encoded with her individual experience, values, attitudes, language, and so on. The receiver hears the message and, from his own perspective (i.e., using his experience, values, attitudes, and language), interprets the message. The receiver provides feedback based on what he believes he has heard.

Too little information may cause a negative reaction, so always keep the receiver in mind when composing the message, whether written or spoken. State the main points succinctly, providing sufficient information regarding an action requested, but not stuffing the message with more information than the person needs.

Note the difference between these two statements:

"All team members will work overtime until further notice."

"Due to the latest information on the market opportunities for this toy, it will be necessary for all team members to work overtime for the next ten days to get the design completed. Thanks for your cooperation."

The first statement is quite likely to create resistance. The receivers of this message have no idea why you are telling them to work overtime or how long they are expected to work these extra hours. Many questions, at least in their minds, surface. Team members will spend time discussing the message and speculating on the answers to their questions. While the second statement takes about seven seconds longer to deliver, the clarity of it allows receivers to hear it and have at least some of their questions answered. They will hear and accept it with less resistance.

"Ann," the office manager for a forty-person trade association, sent an e-mail to all staff members stating that new Apple computers would be installed the following week. Although most people agreed they needed new computers, almost no one liked the abruptness of the change or the choice of brand, which represented a real departure from the personal computers they had on their desks. Ann would not have encountered such initial hostility if she'd simply told the staff that she had to act fast to get a big discount and that the purchase included two days of training with flexible dates.

Questioning Styles

Clear communication involves asking good questions as much as it does making statements. The four basic types of questions are open-ended, closed-ended, probing, and hypothetical. (Advantages and examples of each as they pertain to the interview process are provided in Chapter 3 in the section on "the hiring process—interviewing.") Knowing the generic value of each type of question will help you choose the right style to use in day-to-day communication, both oral and written.

Open-Ended Questions

- ➜ Open-ended questions require full multiple-word responses.

- ➜ The answers generally lend themselves to discussion and result in information that you can use to build additional questions.

- ➜ Open-ended questions thus allow you time to plan subsequent questions.

- ➜ Open-ended questions encourage people to talk, which gives you an opportunity to listen actively to responses, assess the other person's verbal communication skills, and observe the individual's pattern of nonverbal communication.

➤ Such questions are especially helpful in encouraging shy or withdrawn employees to talk.

Example: *"What are some of the ways you might use that speaker's information on rapport building?"*

Closed-Ended Questions

➤ Closed-ended questions are answered with a single word— generally yes or no.

➤ Because closed-ended questions result in concise answers, they give the questioner greater control than open-ended questions.

Example: *"Do you plan to use the speaker's techniques for rapport building?"*

Probing Questions

➤ Probing questions move a conversation along by building on a previous statement.

➤ They are usually short and simply worded.

➤ There are three types of probing questions:

1. **Rational probes** request reasons, using short questions such as "Why?" "How?" "When?" "How often?" and "Who?"

   Example*: "How will you use the speaker's information on rapport building?"*

2. **Clarifier probes** are used to qualify or expand upon information provided in a previous response, using questions such as, "What caused that to happen?" "Who else was involved in that decision?" "What happened next?" and "What were the circumstances that led to that result?"

> **Example:** *"What are some of the other ways you might use the speaker's information?"*

3. **Verifier probes** check out the honesty of a statement.

> **Example:** *"You said in your e-mail that your new rapport-building skills have already made a difference in your sales efforts. Can you quantify the impact?"*

➡ People who have trouble providing full answers usually appreciate the extra help that comes from a probing question, but too many probing questions can make them feel defensive.

Hypothetical Questions

➡ Hypothetical questions are based on anticipated situations and pose a problem.

➡ Hypotheticals help you assess some of the personality traits and idiosyncrasies in people's work styles that could make a big difference in a project.

> **Example:** *Before going into a meeting with a potential customer, you might ask your direct report, "If the customer seems uncomfortable with the discussion, what are some of the ways you might put him more at ease?"*

Elements of Communication

The companion issue to what constitutes important communication is how to communicate it. Paying attention to the words selected and the way in which they may be received is critical for effective communication. Once the message has been delivered, look and ask for feedback. Feedback can be verbal or visual, and it is necessary. For example, if you deliver the message in person and see the other person (the receiver of the message) looking anxious or slightly turning away, the feedback through body language is that of discomfort or resistance. The e-mail equivalent would be a note with a defensive tone, or perhaps a very short note that seems to have "attitude." Revisit what you said and how you said it to determine how your message might have provoked that kind of response.

Consider the three major elements of communication in refining your communication style:

1. **Verbal**—the words we choose.

2. **Vocal**—the way we say them (i.e., voice tone, pitch, volume).

3. **Visual**—body language, facial expressions, eye movement, gesturing.

Each of these components contributes to the overall effectiveness of communication. If you are able to use all three elements, you will have the greatest chance to be understood. When you are able to use only one or two, you will have the greatest chance to be misunderstood.

E-mail and texting probably present the greatest challenges in terms of averting misinterpretation of a message, since neither captures the person's tone of voice or provides visual feedback. To escalate the challenge even more, e-mail and texting can both serve as informal communication in addition to purposeful business communication, with texting having the added aura of being "urgent." One more complication: They are one-way communications. Even exchanged in rapid sequence, text messages are not exactly interactive (as a real-time phone or face-to-face discussion would be). Even instant messaging is neither as instant as a face-to-face exchange, nor as complete as another interactive exchange with all of the vocal and visual elements evident.

Of course, used well, texting and IMing can be ideal communications tools for business. Matt Feeney, president of Creative Engineering Solutions, uses texting to help coordinate installations of solar panels at client sites. He succinctly and silently sends dispatch orders and answers questions from installers (even those working from other client sites) during breaks at meetings. It's a much more efficient, private, and courteous means of communicating than having a loud "Can you hear me now?" cell phone conversation.

The fundamental problem with a one-way communication channel, though, is that it prevents the speaker and the listener from being able to easily identify confusion during the communication process. Typically, in a face-to-face or phone discussion, you are able to see or hear this confusion and can alleviate it by furnishing additional information or adopting different body language or another tone of voice. It is imperative, therefore, that you send the message from the perspective of the receiver so that, regardless of the mood or situation of the receiver, the message is understood as you intend it to be.

And if you broadcast a message, as e-mail, for instance, how can you ascertain whether you've connected with the perspective of those different recipients? All too often, people craft their e-mails for the person or set of people (such as members of a project team) who require the information being transmitted. And then, at the last minute perhaps, they cc the boss and another department manager because they "might be interested."

Consider whether all these people really need to see the message. Even consider your boss's need to know. People in business spend hours opening, reading, and acting on e-mails. Many of these hours are unnecessarily spent because the messages are not relevant to the recipient. You can influence how people use their time by being more discriminating when addressing your e-mail messages and including only those people who have a need to know. As you become discriminating in selecting your addressees, you can also become influential in minimizing unwanted e-mails directed to you by responding to the senders and asking them to eliminate you from their list for that topic.

Because e-mail is permanent and can easily be forwarded, it is important to take care in composing the message. Respect the fact that e-mail is today's equivalent of the business letter, so reread every one before hitting the "send" button to ensure that your grammar, punctuation, and spelling meet good business communication standards. In addition to those basics, follow the etiquette of electronic communication, which tracks with the good manners of any written communication:

- → Think before you write.

- → Avoid "flaming" or expressing extreme emotion.

- → Read your messages carefully before sending them.

- → Stick to your subject.

PURPOSEFUL COMMUNICATION— THE SKILL IN SERVICE

Consider how you might respond to two e-mails, one of which comes from your manager and one of which comes from a member of your team. The first asks you to cut your department budget by 10 percent. The second enthusiastically proposes a course of action that reflects a misunderstanding about department goals. Your purpose in responding to both is to demonstrate cooperation and avoid misunderstanding, but each reply takes shape quite differently.

Using Communication to Manage Up

An important application of your ability to communicate effectively is using your skill to manage up. You may often be caught between your boss's thinking and your own thinking and that of your staff. It is easy to assume that the person who promoted you has more knowledge and better ideas than you do, but that person may not have knowledge about the people who report to you, or the work in which you are currently involved.

Take all of that into consideration when responding to the "cut 10 percent" request. A typical e-mail response would be to say that you will comply; then go back to your desk and take a hard look at how to do that. However, if you know that a budget cut will affect your team's ability to meet its objectives for the year, it would be better to ask your boss for more information about the priorities of your objectives and what must be retained and what can be delayed or eliminated. By doing so, you get your boss to buy into the new priorities, or possibly reduce the cuts that must be made.

Purposeful communication, in this example, reflects thinking through big-picture considerations. Blindly obedient compliance with the request to cut, however, shows that you fall short in playing the role of manager-as-leader.

Communicating Organizational Goals

In the second case, you need to find an effective way to communicate organizational goals to your employee—without dampening the enthusiasm that came through in the employee's e-mail. A starting point is focusing the employee on the intersection of her interests and the organization's. The proposal for action may engage the employee in using talents and skills currently underutilized, for example. In explaining what the organization needs are and what your department aims to accomplish to achieve that end, explore with the employee how those talents and skills can play a part. (There is more on the specific topic of setting objectives to achieve goals in Chapter 2 on Performance Management.)

Running Effective Meetings

Meetings require sustained, purposeful communication. The first rule of running a good meeting, then, is that it have a purpose. If anyone at the table has a legitimate concern and has to ask "Why are we here?" then the manager running the meeting loses ground with his direct reports.

Other common complaints about meetings include:

→ They start late.

→ There's no clear objective for the meeting.

➜ The meeting is disorganized.

➜ Some attendees don't participate.

➜ Some attendees do all the talking.

➜ They run longer than they need to be.

➜ There's no common understanding of the results.

Approaching the meeting in a logical, organized manner is the key to success. There are four steps you can take to help ensure that your meeting is effective:

1. Planning the meeting

2. Announcing the meeting

3. Conducting the meeting

4. Evaluating the meeting

Keep in mind that a meeting fits into the category of communication, so these same steps are valuable reminders of the critical components of any type of communication, including those things you write or say as well. In essence, you want to determine what you're going to communicate, make it clear to the recipient what you will talk or write about, effect the communication, and then figure out whether you got the message across.

Step 1: Planning
Consider these factors in planning your meeting:

Purpose: What results do you want from the meeting?

Agenda: What topics will be discussed? In what order? In how much depth?

Length: When should the meeting be held and how long should it last?

Attendees: Who should attend? (Make sure the right individuals are included.)

Evaluation: How will you know the meeting has been successful?

Notice, too, that the first three factors (purpose, agenda, and length) constitute the PAL formula for good meeting planning.

Step 2: Announcing

Give people written notice of the meeting in an e-mail, text message, or memo. Just passing someone in the hall and mentioning that there is a meeting next Tuesday will not suffice. In your written notice, include the agenda. Having an agenda helps everyone plan for the meeting and keeps them focused on the meeting's purpose. Your advance agenda should also include additional information that will help prepare others for their participation in the meeting.

Use the PAL formula to let people know about the meeting. For example:

Please plan to attend a staff meeting in the conference room on Tuesday, June 24 at 10:00 a.m. Be prepared to discuss the following topic in detail. Please bring all ideas with you.

Purpose: To develop a process to introduce the new software system to the entire organization.

Agenda:

1. Introductions

2. Current status of the software system

3. Discussion of the process required for the software introduction

4. Identification of who will be involved

5. Development of target dates

6. Assignment of responsibilities

7. Next steps

8. Meeting evaluation

Length: 4 hours. Lunch will be provided.

Step 3: Conducting

By definition, a meeting means coming together. By connotation, it suggests the interaction of those who have come together. Keep that in mind and avoid domination or "information dump" by any single individual. All participants want and need a chance to talk about their ideas and help develop solutions for the meeting purpose. Ask yourself: If someone sitting at the table has nothing to contribute, then why is he there?

Tips for Productive Meetings

→ Start the meeting with general information about the purpose. This gives everyone a common foundation from which to begin the communication.

→ Establish some "meeting-keeping" roles. These roles include timekeeper, agenda cop, scribe, and moderator. This will help ensure that the meeting runs smoothly and that meeting notes will be available for everyone.

→ Have a mechanism for retaining good off-topic ideas. One approach is to have the person write the thought on a piece of paper and hand it to the agenda cop for inclusion at the appropriate moment. Another is to have the participant put the thought on a Post-it note and place it on a whiteboard designated as a "parking lot" for ideas. In this way, the thought is acknowledged and not forgotten.

→ Follow the agenda.

→ Generate discussion among all attendees. Ways to do this include:

- Ask for feedback.

- Ask another attendee to paraphrase what was just said.

- Encourage participation by asking quiet attendees what they think.

- Reflect what you think is being said or thought.

- Support participants' ideas.

→ Recap the outcomes or results of the meetings. Make sure that all attendees know the action expected of them, based on the meeting's discussions.

→ Meet your time commitments. If the meeting is running late, ask participants if they are able to extend the time, or reschedule the meeting continuation for another time.

→ Review "parking lot" items. If possible within the originally scheduled time, address these contributions. If time will not permit, ask if another meeting needs to be scheduled with these items on the agenda.

→ Set a time for a next meeting. If another meeting is required to achieve the stated purpose, establish the time before everyone leaves. Never set a meeting unless it's necessary and the most efficient way to accomplish a task, though.

Step 4: Evaluating

Asking participants for a meeting evaluation can accomplish a few important things, and it does not need to be a formal evaluation, written like a report, to have benefit. First, participants might point out that certain other people should be included in the next discussion. Second, it could yield ideas on enhancing the agenda.

The other major benefits—that is, finding out what participants thought went right or went wrong in the meeting—generally come out of anonymous feedback. A feedback form used to collect anonymous contributions can elicit very helpful information on what people think could be done differently to improve the next meeting. If you choose to use a formal evaluation, consider the value of a meeting evaluation form that asks for both ratings and a brief narrative response. For example:

1. How well did the meeting achieve its stated objectives?

   1 = Not at all; **2** = A little; **3** = Somewhat; **4** = Fairly well; **5** = Completely

2. How well did the meeting achieve your personal objectives?

   1 = Not at all; **2** = A little; **3** = Somewhat; **4** = Fairly well; **5** = Completely

3. What parts of the meeting helped you most to do your job?

   a. _____

   b. _____

   c. _____

4. Which ones helped you least?

   a. _____

   b. _____

   c. _____

5. What actions will you take as a result of the meeting?

6. Other comments?

When you get feedback from your employees, use it. If a keen insight comes out of an evaluation, make it clear through action and open acknowledgment that the change you're making came about because of someone's good idea.

CHAPTER 2

Performance Management

Effective performance management is the avenue for achieving organizational goals that impact the bottom line of the business. Master the skill and you will be able to create a greater alignment of the organization's interests and those of the individual employees.

THE PROCESS OF MANAGING

A process for managing the performance and development of your direct reports equips you to carry out your primary responsibility of getting work done through others.

Any performance management system is supported by critical skills that are necessary for both you and your direct reports to be successful. So, regardless of what particular system your organization relies on, the skills and tools described in this section will support your efforts to implement it. Simply overlay what you learn here with the system you use in your organization.

To start, let's get specific about what performance management is and is not.

Performance Management Is...

→ An ongoing process of working with your direct reports in a partnership for the purpose of helping them (and you) be successful

→ An ongoing communication for the benefit of the organization and the individual

Performance Management Is Not...

→ A once-a-year appraisal

→ An opportunity to punish or intimidate your direct reports

You need a plan to ensure that you achieve the "is" while avoiding the trap of the "is not." You risk falling into the trap if you let performance management slip as a priority. Most companies set expectations or objectives at the beginning, or near the beginning, of the calendar or fiscal year. Some of these objectives are set from the top down, and others are set up from the individual contributor level. However your company sets objectives, it is important that your direct reports agree to those objectives that they will own.

Review periods are also set by policy in most companies. Some companies require only an annual review; others require two, three, or four reviews annually. Regardless of the number of required reviews in your company, you may choose to hold more performance discussions than that number. Experts in the performance management field recommend that reviews be held at least quarterly so that individuals have the opportunity to get back on track if they have strayed off course.

Often, the most difficult step to take in putting together performance management plans is the first step—that is, to set objectives or expectations. The next big challenge comes in having review meetings. Managers often balk at the prospect of working on performance management plans. They have a litany of excuses starting with "I don't have time" and moving to "It's just an administrative requirement" and "It's not an important part of my job."

If you keep one thing in mind, you can move past procrastination and resistance and get the process moving: You and your direct report are the team that gives the process energy and meaning. Many managers think that they must do all of the work in the development of the performance management plan. But when the manager and the direct report share responsibilities, development of the plan becomes much more approachable. No manager should feel that she is operating independently when it comes to an individual's performance. After all, it is the individual's job that is being affected, and the individual needs to take ownership for her success in that job.

Provide a clear framework for developing objectives so that your direct reports are in sync with you on how to express them. Well-written objectives follow the format of being SMART:

Specific

Measurable

Attainable

Relevant

Trackable and Time-bound

Once the objectives are written and agreed upon, tracking the results becomes an ongoing process. A review of the progress in meeting the objectives provides the opportunity for the direct report to ask for support and the manager to understand what to do to help the individual achieve the required results.

Examples of well-written objectives are as follows:

"Increase sales of project management software applications by 10 percent by end of year."

"Train five departments on the use of the new expense reimbursement process in the third quarter of this year."

"Reduce data-entry errors from previous quarterly results by 3 percent each quarter of this year."

"Complete six days of security training by end of year."

Setting objectives is the beginning of the continuous process of performance management. The middle involves ongoing conversations and meetings, at least quarterly, to discuss progress on expectations and identify what level of support is needed for successful achievement of stated objectives. The final appraisal is the end. And the way to keep track of everything your direct reports do is by keeping records.

Following is an example of a report, prepared quarterly, that incorporates practical guidance and useful insights for both the reviewing manager and the employee.

QUARTERLY EMPLOYEE PERFORMANCE REVIEW

Conducted by: Jane Smiley

Date: June 30, 2011

Employee Information

Employee Name: Victor Hardy	**Employee ID:** 12345
Job Title: Copy Editor	**Start Date:** November 16, 2009

Department: Marketing

Review Period: 3/31 to 6/30

Reviewer Reminders

Did you notify the employee of the review at least a week in advance?

Did you ask the employee to do a self-review?

If not, reschedule the review.

Goals

What were the goals for the period? Were they achieved? If yes, what contributed to the success? If no, why not?

Goal #1: Take seminar in current legal issues.

Yes, but felt presenter wasn't adequately prepared to address questions related to the company's key foreign market. Recommends shift to webinars with panelists who can cover broader set of questions.

Goal #2: Show more confidence in core strength by rewriting when necessary.

Only a little progress. Feels as though others have more talent. Needs coaching, so won't be held back from promotion because now showing initiative.

Goal #3: Research reasons for changing or retaining house style.

Yes. Excellent job of analysis. Conclusion: Continues to excel in tasks requiring little or no teamwork, but as soon as interaction with others comes into play, he pulls back.

A non-narrative evaluation can also help both the employee and manager as long as they have a mutual understanding of evaluation criteria and the rating system. Just as you no doubt experienced in school, on the job there will sometimes be "harsh graders" who almost never give high marks. If a system like the following one is used, it's best to have more than one evaluator, as well as to invite the employee to use the form to do a self-evaluation.

Evaluation

Use this rating key for the following evaluation:

1 =   Unsatisfactory
Fails to do the required tasks and/or undermines the work of others.

2 =   Marginal
Needs improvement. Gets the job done, but tends to miss deadlines and/or have deficits in quality.

3 =   Meets Requirements
Meets basic requirements. Gets the job done on time and meets quality requirements.

4 =   Exceeds Requirements
On a regular basis, goes above and beyond expectations.

5 =   Exceptional
Consistently gets results far beyond requirements.

	5	4	3	2	1
Achieves Established Goals					
Responds to Coaching					
Demonstrates Required Skills					
Completes Assigned Tasks					
Shows Accountability					
Calls Out Potential Problems					
Tries to Solve Problems					
Offers Suggestions to Improve					
Generates Creative Ideas					

Tools of Managing

Your personnel records serve as a primary tool in performance management. In most companies, the personnel or human resources department keeps a file for each employee. The manager needs to keep a different type of "personnel file." The manager's file should include all information for individuals that affects their performance evaluations. This information includes the following:

➜ Documentation of all conversations regarding performance.

➜ Written record of comments from customers (internal or external) about the individuals' performance.

➜ Documentation of observations you have made of the individuals.

➜ Letters of commendation.

➜ E-mailed comments on performance or work.

➜ Comments from your manager about the individuals and/or their work.

When it comes to comments from customers, peers, and even other managers, make a careful distinction between hearsay and direct observation or experience, as well as factual assertions and statements that are emotionally charged. An e-mail that claims someone handled a customer situation badly, for example, could reflect the sender's mood and/or a skewed point of view more than the reality of an interaction.

Another tool of performance management is the digital calendar. Four key features make it an almost indispensable tool for today's managers:

1. *Meeting Requests.* The meeting-request feature of a digital calendar provides the ability to both request and receive an appointment with someone else.

2. *Automatic Updates.* Digital calendars have the capacity to grab specific schedules and sync them to a computing device. For example, if you have a training schedule involving direct reports and need to make changes in it, you can feed that information efficiently and update everyone's calendar.

3. *Recurring Events.* Adding these events to the calendar ensures that there are "no excuses" for missing a staff meeting or regular conference call. Built-in alarms sound when the meeting is at hand.

4. *Accessibility.* Since nearly everyone carries a smartphone or other mobile computing device, the efficiency of putting calendar information on the device surpasses putting it on paper.

Using digital tools as part of the performance management process reinforces the sense of connection that you want with direct reports. It reduces the chance of people misunderstanding when team meetings or sessions or private discussions with individuals are scheduled to occur.

In performance management, it's easy to see how the leader, director, observer, and organizer roles of the manager come into play. This next section focuses more on your roles as contributor and coach.

FUNDAMENTALS OF MOTIVATION

Some managers view motivation as a polite word for describing what they perceive as their authority or power position: "Whether or not you like it, I'm going to get you to do what I want you to do." You may get results in the short term, but the long-term impact of that approach to motivating direct reports leads to resentment, hostility, and demotivation. The only motivation that truly works is self-motivation. You cannot force someone else to be motivated. What you can provide is an environment in which an individual feels genuinely motivated.

Herzberg's Model

Frederick Herzberg, a behavioral scientist and author of *The Motivation to Work*, developed a motivation theory specifically for the workplace. Herzberg's motivator-hygiene theory contains two sets of factors: those related to preventing dissatisfaction (hygiene factors) and those related to engendering satisfaction (motivation factors).

Hygiene, or Maintenance, Factors

→ Pay

→ Status

→ Security

→ Working conditions

→ Fringe benefits

→ Policies and administrative practices

Herzberg states that, in a work environment, these maintenance factors relate to the context of a job and will tend to eliminate job dissatisfaction if present in proper form for the individual. Though their presence can create short-term job satisfaction and help maintain the organization, they will not necessarily motivate staff. For instance, allowing casual dress may satisfy employees initially. After a short while, though, the privilege will be taken for granted. Maintenance factors do not produce strong, long-term satisfaction or motivation. Requiring standard business dress, on the other hand, may cause employee dissatisfaction and eventually reduce motivation.

Herzberg's work suggests a two-stage process for managing employee satisfaction and motivation.

Stage 1: Addressing the Maintenance Factors

First, managers should address maintenance factors to meet basic needs so that employees do not grow dissatisfied. Managers must make sure employees are adequately paid, that working conditions are safe and clean, that workers have opportunities for social interaction, and that treatment by managers is fair and humane.

These maintenance factors have changed as the workplace has changed. In the past, having an interesting job with adequate compensation and reasonable working conditions was good enough. However, as the workplace has expanded to include many different generations and cultures with different life experiences and expectations, the elements of work that can cause dissatisfaction have changed. Today, maintenance factors such as fringe benefits (e.g., vacation time, work location, work scheduling and hours) should be looked at, so that the employees do not become dissatisfied.

In some cases, these factors are not under your managerial control. Many times, they are negotiated by parties outside of your immediate work group. Nonetheless, when you observe dissatisfaction in a direct report, you need to take action. Ignoring the dissatisfaction will inhibit the progress of motivation or performance improvement. Shrugging your shoulders and sighing, "Can't do a thing about that" will do the same thing.

Work through the dissatisfaction issues to the best of your ability and take the following steps to whatever extent possible:

- → *Acknowledge the situation.* In some instances, paying attention, acknowledging the situation, and discussing it can satisfy a direct report. The fact that you have put the issue out on the table and are willing to hear an individual's concerns can be enough to minimize, and sometimes eliminate, the dissatisfaction.

- → *Communicate.* Many times, employees are not aware of why a policy needs to be changed or office space reduced. Be available for questions and explanations. Explaining why a situation has occurred and discussing it with staff provides understanding and often alleviates dissatisfaction.

→ *Work toward a solution.* Meeting with a direct report and jointly charting a course are important actions. Beyond acknowledging a situation, discussing a plan to move toward resolving the issue (if feasible) may be required to minimize or eliminate dissatisfaction.

→ *Take action.* Sometimes taking action and getting results are the only ways to satisfy a direct report. If action is not a realistic option, then communicate that fact.

Because of Herzberg's belief that maintenance factors are not motivators, he concentrates on what managers can do to address the needs of individuals related to the achievement of their own self-esteem and confidence.

Motivational Factors

→ *Achievement*—Work must provide the opportunity for individuals to gain a sense of achievement. The job must have a beginning and an end, and have a product of some sort.

→ *Responsibility*—In order for the achievement to be felt, the individual must feel responsible for the work.

→ *Meaningfulness*—The work must be meaningful to the individual in order to promote motivation, or at least the work environment must be meaningful.

→ *Recognition*—This motivator should be used extensively to ensure that direct reports know their managers are aware of their accomplishments.

→ *Opportunities for growth and advancement*—These conditions must exist for the individual to be motivated.

Perry Ellsworth ran the two-person office of the National Council of Agricultural Employers in downtown Washington, D.C. Because the organization had no intent to grow the size of the office, his executive assistant had no chance of getting a promotion of substance, nor did she want it. Upon being hired, she made a three-year commitment to do her best for the organization while she went to graduate school part-time. Perry boosted her motivation by giving her credit for accomplishments in writing and in front of the board of directors; taking a hands-off approach for tasks she owned; keeping her informed of his incremental lobbying victories to make life easier for farmers; respecting her office space instead of barging in when he needed something; and allowing her to create a schedule that enabled her to attend afternoon, as well as evening, classes. When she left the organization after four years, having earned her master's degree, her resignation letter said she was sorry to leave Perry Ellsworth, the Gerber Baby, and the Jolly Green Giant, three of her favorite faces in agriculture. Not for a moment did she hate her job or resent going to work, even though her field of study was theater.

Stage 2: Addressing the Motivational Factors
Your staff members need to experience the internal motivators that drive them to success. Because these natural motivators are internal and subjective, what is naturally motivating to one person may be different for another. These motivators are tied to job outcomes or the tasks associated with the work environment.

Countering Workplace Dissatisfaction

Looking more closely at the motivators that were previously listed, you can see that there are some specific issues that may impact the motivation level of your individual direct reports. In the following table, the checklist on the left will help in evaluating what might be missing from the work of our direct reports. The companion actions on the right address ways of mitigating and solving the problems at the root of dissatisfaction.

MOTIVATIONAL CHECKLIST	COMPANION ACTIONS
ACHIEVEMENT	**ACTIONS**
Is there an opportunity for a sense of completion?	Set and monitor goals on an ongoing basis.
Are there goals and targets to which individuals can relate? Is there a sense of ownership?	Provide ongoing feedback on goal achievement.
Is there a plan in place for ongoing feedback? Can the person measure any progress in attaining goals?	If goals are in jeopardy, discuss them with your direct report and provide support and suggestions on meeting the goals. Look for the intersection of the organization's goals and the individual's career goals.
Does this job require a person to learn more or to develop more technical knowledge and expertise?	If there are no hard benchmarks (for example, those involving cost, time, or quality), then develop a system of gauging progress that makes sense to you and the employee. 　　When people resist taking on a new job, build in learning time and success factors. Individuals who fear failure will resist new jobs. Offer training opportunities—in-house or from an outside source. 　　Offer your direct report the opportunity to team up with someone else to learn a new skill.
RESPONSIBILITY	**ACTIONS**
Is there a degree of freedom in the job?	Provide opportunities for your direct report to be visible and/or influential.
Are people in control of their own behavior?	Ask for advice, opinions, and suggestions, and follow up by responding to them as appropriate.
Is there a degree of risk involved?	Risk can invite people to take initiative and to think creatively, as long as failure is treated as a learning experience rather than an automatic cause for censure.
Do your direct reports have the authority to make decisions and solve problems on their own? Do they direct the work of others? Are they accountable for important resources?	Delegate—that is, provide opportunities for your direct reports to organize and direct an activity.

Cont'd.

MOTIVATIONAL CHECKLIST	COMPANION ACTIONS
RECOGNITION	**ACTIONS**
Is there an opportunity for visibility?	Provide opportunities for a direct report to work with others when possible. Provide opportunities for the direct report to be visible in a positive way. Establish a relationship that provides feedback and attention.
Is there an opportunity for recognition by management? Do accomplishments get noticed or publicized?	Remember that a simple "thank you" that specifies why you're grateful (e.g., for completing work on time, under budget, or of high quality) goes a long way.
MEANINGFULNESS	**ACTIONS**
Is performing this job a preparation for higher levels of responsibility? Or is it good training for moving laterally?	Employees get frustrated with tasks that keep them treading water. Work with each direct report to find a task, or aspect of a task, that involves professional growth.
Is the job or assignment challenging?	Vary assignments enough so that the employee doesn't feel as if the same skill is all that's necessary for each task.
Does the work have value in and of itself?	Occasionally remind the employee of how a task or project helps the organization drive toward achieving the mission.
Does the job allow for personal growth?	As part of the periodic review, ask the employee to rate recent assignments in terms of value to advancing career development and improving interpersonal skills.
Does it increase the employee's self-confidence?	Ask the employee what would make work more meaningful.
Does it improve the employee's ability to work with others?	Offer the employee an opportunity to cross-train. Give direct reports a chance to take on a new responsibility as part of their duties.

MOTIVATIONAL CHECKLIST	COMPANION ACTIONS
OPPORTUNITIES FOR GROWTH AND ADVANCEMENT	ACTIONS
Can employees learn from their work?	Ask employees about their career objectives.
Is promotion (lateral or vertical) possible?	Find cross-training and rotational opportunities for employees.
Can employees learn new skills? Will others in the organization see the results of your employees' work?	Provide training opportunities to employees on a subject they want to learn, so they can progress in the organization.

Uncovering Employees' Motivators

Using these questions as a guide, observe your direct reports to determine whether their needs are being met. Then, ask them these questions; be direct so that they have the chance to tell you what's working and what isn't. Remember that asking questions in a supportive way shows that you care about the individual and want to use the information you learn in positive ways.

Once you identify the motivational factors, take actions, such as those suggested in the previous table, to address them. Work with other people, if necessary, to determine what changes can be made to increase motivation. Provide the environment, direction, and support for the given situation, and the motivation will come on its own. Motivation is a key performance management concept because, by creating a motivational environment, you help improve your employees' performance.

Providing your direct reports with the right environment, with the right amount of direction and support, will increase the potential for having motivated individuals on your team. Your ability to coach and delegate will enable your employees to grow in competence and strengthen their commitment to the work they do for your organization. All of these factors strongly influence their motivation.

DELEGATION FOR GROWTH AND DEVELOPMENT

Delegation allows another individual or group to work on a project or task that offers motivation and rewards on its successful completion. It also offers the manager the opportunity to grow and develop individuals who can then be recognized as high-level contributors in the organization.

Begin your close look into the practice of delegating with a self-assessment on your comfort level with delegation. This self-assessment is included as Appendix A.

Two-Way Benefits of Delegating

Managers can and should delegate with employees who have the necessary skills and enthusiasm to take on an additional project or task and who see it as an opportunity. Coaching employees to improve their skill and knowledge levels can be accomplished through effective delegation.

Managers who delegate effectively have direct reports who are more capable and enthusiastic because of their delegation experience. They are seen as competent and committed to taking on more projects or tasks, thereby freeing up the manager's time to work on tasks that cannot be delegated.

Managers who either do not delegate or do so halfheartedly or haphazardly run a high risk of having a demoralized and demotivated workforce who will not improve their skill or knowledge levels. Keep in mind that accomplishing work through others is the manager's primary job; therefore delegation is a key performance management tool. Consider this story:

> *A large, not-for-profit museum had five people devoted to fund-raising. For the first few years, the museum's chief executive managed the group directly, but as the museum grew she eventually saw that her other responsibilities precluded her from doing a good job. She hired a director for all development efforts. Productivity problems arose and became*

obvious to the CEO. In conducting a performance evaluation, the CEO asked each member of the director's staff: "What's it like working with Janet?" She quickly found the answer to the productivity problem. Janet's background in institutional fund-raising naturally drew her to second-guess and "correct" the efforts of the three development officers doing corporate, foundation, and government fund-raising. She left the officers for events planning and individual donations alone since their areas of operation seemed foreign to her. She also took a hands-off approach with the department's administrative aide, since she wasn't interested in what that person did. When the CEO told Janet of her findings, Janet was shocked. She honestly thought she was helping the institutional fund-raisers, not getting in their way. As soon as she made a real attempt at delegating, the productivity problem faded away.

Until you involve others, you will probably struggle with your role as a manager. You will feel like you have more tasks than time to do them. You may feel overwhelmed by the workload and responsibilities. You may even hate coming in to work because facing the day is so difficult.

Regardless of the strong personal reasons to share the workload with your competent and committed employees, there are also many business reasons to learn to delegate. Among them are these:

→ More work can be accomplished.

→ Direct reports become more involved.

→ Remote locations can be more effectively managed.

→ Development of direct reports occurs as part of the process.

→ It is cost-effective for the company.

In spite of these compelling arguments to delegate, a surprising number of new managers avoid it. They have a fear that delegating will put the glory of the accomplishment on someone other than them, or worry that they are the only ones who really know how to do the job, so it would be "wrong" to hand it over to another person. Corollary reasons are that they don't have faith in their employees' abilities or simply don't have the patience to describe the task requirements to other people and figure it's easier to do it themselves. Another common reason is simple lack of experience in delegating. They just do not know how to get started.

The Process of Delegating

The following steps may help you overcome any resistance you have to delegation because the process itself is foreign.

Five Steps to Delegation Success

1. Analyze the task.

    - Determine the existing situation. Is it a component of a larger effort or the next step in a series?

    - Realistically establish how soon the task needs to be completed. Projects without extraordinary time constraints are inherently a better fit for delegating than those with tight schedules.

    - Determine the budget and available resources. The word *available* has a lot of significance, because the organization may have resources that aren't available to the particular task or to someone who isn't a manager, for example.

    - Identify specific, measurable goals.

2. Select a delegatee.

    - Identify the knowledge and skills needed to carry out the task.

- Match the job requirements to the delegatee. In some cases, the employee's previous job may have prepared the person to assume responsibility for a task, so take work history into consideration.

- Establish any needed training and support. Most people prefer to learn to dive by being taught, rather than being pushed off a cliff.

- Estimate checkpoints.

3. Assign the task.

- Describe the task and the goals. To the greatest extent possible, put the goals in the context of the organization's mission.

- Tell the delegatee specifically why you selected him. In making your selection, you may have made assumptions about the person's capabilities and interests. Citing the specifics of your choice gives your delegatee an opening to clarify what he thinks he would do well.

- Be specific about responsibilities and authority. If the person is allowed to share the task or "sub-delegate," be clear about that.

4. Execute the task.

- Share the delegatee's level of authority with other staff members. Make sure the person is never in the uncomfortable position of trying to exercise authority no one knows she has.

- Keep the delegatee informed of issues and circumstances that could affect performance.

5. Conduct regularly scheduled feedback sessions.

- Uncover problems early. Even a quick status update can help you flag troublesome issues or aspects of the task that may have been ill-conceived.

When to Delegate—and When Not To

Just because you know the process of delegating does not mean you should jump into it. Differentiating between tasks that can and should be delegated and tasks that require personal handling is just as important as knowing how to delegate. Consider the contrasts between examples of work that can effectively be given to others and work that needs to remain on your turf:

Assignments That Probably Can Be Delegated

→ Tasks closely related to the work employees are already doing.

→ Tasks with clearly defined procedures and end results.

→ Repetitive tasks that fit into the normal work flow.

→ Tasks that enable employees to develop themselves.

Any one of these examples could turn into a task that probably should not be delegated, however, if the time frame for completion puts extreme pressure on the individual. Consider this story:

"Julia" is a young woman who took a job with a Madison Avenue advertising firm right after graduating with honors from college. Her boss delegated an inordinate amount of assignments to her because she was intelligent and thorough. She could have handled the work if she could have paced herself, but in order to meet expectations, she needed to work evenings and weekends. One Saturday afternoon, she broke down. Julia stormed out of the office crying and promptly got on a train headed south to her parents' home.

Some personality types thrive under that kind of pressure. Many others do not. As a manager, you need to pay attention to how your direct reports respond to the tasks you delegate.

Circumstances When Delegation May Be Inappropriate

- Tasks are of a highly sensitive nature (e.g., salary reviews, disciplinary actions).
- Tasks are not clearly defined or some uncertainty about a task exists.
- When tasks involve decision making, higher-up management expects the manager to handle them.
- Resources are severely limited, whether they are human resources, equipment, or funding.

A task that managers commonly delegate, which may or may not be appropriate to have a surrogate handle, is the "thanks for a job well done." You should always take the time to express gratitude yourself to the individual or the group of people who performed well. However, when the expression of gratitude comes in the form of a party, for example, delegating is a reasonable option.

COACHING TO BOOST PERFORMANCE

Coaching is the process of creating the environment and building the relationships that enhance the development of skills and the performance of both the direct reports and the manager. Jim McCormick, professional coach and coauthor of the sixth edition of *The First-Time Manager* (AMACOM), summarizes the process as follows: "At its core, coaching is about identifying the existing situation and the desired one and then helping the team member to plot and travel the path to get from the first to the second."

A vital part of a manager's contribution to a culture of continuous learning, motivation, and growth, coaching helps to improve performance as well as reduce workplace concerns. For instance, you may find that there are times when you need to coach your direct reports on issues that are not task- or commitment-related but that definitely influence the environment and the relationships within your work group. A direct report may need a little coaching on business dress, for example, if the senior executive conducting a meeting would rather see suits than blue jeans.

Coaching is one of a manager's key skills for engendering high performance among employees. Working in complement, the performance management skills of coaching and delegating will help you do what a manager is paid to do—that is, achieve results with and through others.

Occasions for Coaching

The reasons for coaching and the circumstances wherein the process takes shape are clear. In today's changing workplace, coaching is the favored strategy for developing individuals because the requirement to do more with fewer resources can only be met if managers broaden their direct reports' responsibilities, help them work more autonomously, and stimulate initiative in solving problems.

There are several practical reasons for coaching:

- *Total Quality Management.* The first-line manager's role is to be a coach rather than an overseer. Coaching provides support to direct reports by helping them develop solutions to problems, rather than by telling them what to do.

- *Structure of Organizations.* Flat organizations have created increased areas of control so that the manager must be more of a coach than a director of specific work activities in order to accomplish all goals.

46

→ *Staff Motivation.* Today's employees are less tolerant of an authoritative, controlling management style. As new generations come into the workplace, it will be increasingly important to pay attention to what motivates different people and to offer them the opportunities to become successful.

→ *Organizational Changes.* Organizations are constantly changing. Coaching is particularly important in a global economy with heightened customer expectations and increased competition.

The Process of Coaching

The process of coaching can be summarized in five steps:

1. State what you have observed.

2. Wait for a response.

3. Remind employees of the goal.

4. Ask for specific solutions.

5. Agree on the solution.

The Mechanics of Coaching

Coaching requires a level of preparation that managers often underestimate. The sessions should not have an ad hoc quality, leaving the direct report wondering how seriously to take the whole thing. As Jim McCormick suggests, the coaching process is about developing a strategy for a course of action as opposed to throwing out ideas for improvement. Taking the necessary time to plan for a coaching meeting will have a major impact on its effectiveness. The little time it takes will pay off by providing a clear understanding of what you want to accomplish.

The first consideration is logistical, so these to-do items need to be handled up front, not on the run:

➤ *Set up a time* with your direct report that is convenient for both of you. It is important that each of you be able to pay attention to the conversation. If other work or personal issues distract either person, then it will be difficult to really listen to one another.

➤ *Find a location* that is appropriate for the coaching you will be doing. If the purpose is to correct a performance problem, then it must be done in a private room.

➤ *Identify the desired results of the coaching meeting with your direct reports.* Your meeting will be more effective when you determine what you intend the outcomes to be—not just in the long-term sense, but also in the immediate sense. What ideas, directions, or game plan do you hope the employee will be able to utilize when he leaves the session?

In addition to planning your coaching meeting, it is important to use effective communication techniques while conducting the meeting. This six-step coaching model focuses on the mechanics of effective communication during the meeting.

PLANNING CONSIDERATIONS	COMMUNICATION TECHNIQUES
STEP 1: SET THE STAGE.	
Why hold this meeting? What instigated the need for the meeting? Is it a problem that needs addressing? OR Do you want to offer your direct report an opportunity to take on new responsibilities? Do you simply want to meet to check the status on annual objectives?	**Clarify—Be Specific.** Give clear statements about perceived performance problems without using accusatory language. Identify the problem. Outline new responsibilities. Scope the related problem. **Limit statements to a single problem or two closely related problems.** Discuss why it is important that changes occur. **Be Future-Oriented.** State the desired change; do not request reasons for failure.
STEP 2: FORMULATE AND FOCUS THE ISSUES.	
What is happening? What questions will you ask to determine what is really happening? What is your direct report thinking? How will you determine what the causes of any problems might be?	**Promote Self-Discovery.** Ask questions to draw out what is happening. Discover the possibilities. **Pay Attention.** Listen actively. Don't interrupt. **Acknowledge.** Give verbal and nonverbal cues indicating your involvement in the conversation. **Gather Information.** Ask questions, acknowledge, probe, reflect, and summarize. *Cont'd.*

PLANNING CONSIDERATIONS	COMMUNICATION TECHNIQUES
STEP 3: GET AGREEMENT.	
How will you know there is agreement on the situation? What will you look and listen for when discussing the situation? How will you ask for agreement on the problem?	**Confirm.** Close the loop—reach mutual agreement on problems and causes. **Indicate Respect.** Don't ridicule, generalize, or judge. **Affirm.** Comment on your direct report's strengths and positive prospects.
STEP 4: GENERATE POSSIBLE SOLUTIONS AND/OR ALTERNATIVES.	
What approach will you take to meet your objectives? What will you say to encourage your direct report to offer solutions? Will you suggest training for improved or expanded knowledge or, perhaps, partnering with a colleague for growth?	**Brainstorm.** Generate as many solutions or alternatives as possible and avoid being judgmental, no matter what the idea. **Draw Out the Consequences.** Weigh the upside and downside of each alternative. **Decide.** Determine the alternative that best meets the situation.
STEP 5: SET GOALS AND DEVELOP AN ACTION PLAN.	
What are the actions to be taken, and what are the consequences? What actions will you expect your direct report to take as a result of this meeting? Have you made sure to include some specific timelines with the actions? Have you determined what the consequences, positive or negative, will be if your suggestions/requirements are not followed? Is there a new position for the person, or will she be more prepared for a promotion?	**Plan.** Build strategies and agree on follow-up, including milestones and timelines. **Strategize.** Consider training, one-on-one mentoring, coaching, and resources. **Recap.** Review key points to reinforce common understanding and ownership.

PLANNING CONSIDERATIONS	COMMUNICATION TECHNIQUES
STEP 6: MONITOR.	
What will happen next? Are there other actions that will be taken? Will another meeting be scheduled?	**Follow through.** Set up follow-up processes, including details on who, when, and how they are handled.

As a manager, you have the responsibility to be certain that all of your direct reports contribute to their fullest potential. Coaching is how you ensure that will happen. Coach your staff members regularly, whether they are performing at an exceptional level or need to improve their skills or behaviors. The Coaching Planning Worksheet (see Appendix B) provides the structure to plan for either type of a coaching meeting.

CHAPTER 3

Managing Staff Changes

Change in an organization occurs because of strategic and tactical requirements, stakeholder demands, chief executive initiatives, and myriad other reasons. In short, the reality of change can involve relatively small shifts or a complete restructuring of the organization. Although it might seem small in an organization of hundreds, or even thousands, of employees, hiring someone new has the potential to be quite significant—and so can firing someone. For that reason, facilitating changes in staff is an essential management skill.

DEALING WITH CHANGE

The principles of dealing with change of any kind in an organization provide a good basis for helping your direct reports handle staffing changes.

Why is it so difficult for some people to change? The answer lies in understanding what happens during the transition from the old way to the new way. When individuals realize that the change is going to affect them, they often experience fear of the unknown. As a manager, how you help those affected by change will influence their ability to progress to the "new way."

What can you do? The most important element for long-term success is to understand that change is difficult for many people. Once you understand that, then how and what you communicate can make the transition easier.

Some communication guidelines include the following:

→ Acknowledge the difficulty people may be experiencing.

→ Create opportunities for short-term successes.

→ Praise achievements.

→ Clearly identify the "new way"—that is, your new relationship to employees as a result of the changes.

→ Make yourself available often, perhaps by adopting the "management by walking around" method in the workplace.

→ Talk to your direct reports about upcoming change when possible.

→ Involve your staff in decisions about changes if appropriate.

It is also best to keep the number of simultaneous changes to a minimum. Too many changes create chaos, which is debilitating. Try to get one change accepted before overlaying another.

By following these guidelines, and taking into consideration the difficulty others may have with change, you increase your probability of success greatly. Remember, not everyone is excited about the changes that happen at work. Helping people become comfortable with a climate of change is part of your management responsibility.

The emotional cycle of change progresses from denial to resistance to exploration to commitment, according to Dean Hohl, author of *Rangers Lead the Way: The Army Rangers' Guide to Leading Your Organization Through Chaos*. If you can move employees to the exploration stage by communicating reasons for and benefits of the change, then they will ask the questions that move them into the commitment phase. Meetings will fill with ideas about how to make the change work.

REASONS FOR HIRING

When the change involves the addition or removal of an individual from the workforce, people need to know why. A staff change in your organization might be necessitated by "recruitment challenges" that may make it difficult to get the ideal complement of people in any organization.

To summarize, there is one general challenge—the right fit—and five other, more specific recruitment challenges:

→ Fluctuating economy

→ Variable skill levels

→ Loyalty and commitment

→ Outsourcing

→ Personnel expectations

Right Fit

The general challenge is ensuring that the people you hire are the ones that best match your organization's culture and fit in well with the rest of the team. A mismatch between an employee and an organization is reason to move an employee to a more suitable environment, whether inside or outside the organization. When that occurs, finding "the right fit" may dominate recruitment considerations. When thinking about who is the best fit, consider these questions:

→ *What does the organization expect from people?* The story of Julia (see Chapter 2) is a typical one for a Madison Avenue or Wall Street firm in which the culture pushes junior people hard in order to groom them for senior positions. In contrast, the culture of many other organizations centers on work-life balance, and employees who inhabit their cubicles on weekends receive counseling, not encouragement. Consider multiple factors in identifying what your organization expects from its people.

➤ *What are the personal qualities of most people who succeed in your organization?* In addition to "doing the job," evaluate the importance of loyalty, discretion, enthusiasm, and other intangibles that successful employees bring to the workplace daily.

➤ *Which personal qualities easily earn respect and which lead to people becoming isolated?* A start-up electronic medical records company in Torrance, California, hired a couple of experienced programmers to oversee development of the database for recordkeeping. One of them interacted easily with other staff members, but the other programmer seemed glued to her computer. Throughout her eight months with the company, people tried to engage her in conversation and include her in activities outside work. She expressed real enjoyment for her work, but ultimately, she could not sustain a relationship with the company itself because her personal qualities were so much at odds with the rest of the group's. In contrast to that, when Dennis Cloutier took over as vice president of sales for a start-up called WatchGuard Technologies (now a highly successful network security company with more than 400 employees), he wondered if he'd ever fit in. "I'm just a bleach salesman," he would joke, in reference to his previous role in sales at Procter & Gamble. But despite his consumer products background, his personality fit well with the rest of the staff's, nearly all of whom had technology backgrounds.

➤ *How would you describe your organization's culture?* It's important not to confuse "mission" and "culture." A toy company might have an ostensibly playful mission to "create products that make kids laugh," but have an intense, demanding culture and vice versa.

➜ *What is the risk level of your organization?* Risk may be part of your organization's culture and modus operandi, or your organization may be so risk-averse that it scripts everything, from sales presentations to HR practices, to keep the organization "safe."

Here's a story to illustrate the importance of a good fit:

Charlotte hired "Candace" because she had intelligence, the right kind of academic credentials, and an extremely appealing appearance. The problem was that no one else in the thirty-six-person office wanted anything to do with her. Within three months, Charlotte was gone and Maryann replaced her.

On a personal level, Maryann and Candace got along well and had several interests in common. On a professional level, Maryann often saw other staff members' eyes roll when it came to working with Candace, and they'd always ask, "Do you know what Candace just did?" Maryann had a candid session with her direct report about career goals and discovered the source of the mismatch—a very common problem with people occupying their first job out of college. Candace viewed the copyediting position at the trade association as a steppingstone to the job she really wanted: creative work in the field of advertising or marketing. From a technical point of view, she did her job well. But she didn't share the culture or energy for the mission of other staff members. There was no fix for the mismatch; Candace left willingly.

Fluctuating Economy

The global economy, or the economy of a nation, will cycle up and down, but the movement of greatest concern in terms of personnel is within your industry. The rest of the world may be falling apart, but if your industry is thriving, then you and your competitors seek new hires from the same pool of qualified people, and the economy favors employees. In contrast, when competition is fierce—and when isn't it?—and you and your competitors face tight margins with a large pool of workers looking for employment, then the economy favors employers.

When the Economy Favors Applicants

→ Applicants tend to make more demands in terms of perks, working conditions, and hours.

→ Applicants may act on harbored feelings of resentment, resulting in impaired employer-employee relations.

→ Applicants are likely to leave—often with little notice—for jobs that are more in line with their skills, salary expectations, and interests.

→ Employers may resent the shift in power and take a "wait until the tables turn" attitude.

→ Employers may rail against what they perceive to be inflated salary and benefits expectations.

→ Employers sometimes feel pressured to fill positions with new hires they consider less than ideal.

When the Economy Favors Employers

→ Employers tend to be more selective in their hiring practices.

→ Employers are less inclined to respond favorably to applicant demands.

→ Employers are more apt to feel justified in raising the bar on expectations.

→ Applicants are more likely to take jobs they would not ordinarily consider.

➔ Applicants may accept salaries below figures they believe they are worth.

➔ Applicants often agree to unpleasant employment conditions.

Variable Skill Levels

A mismatch between skills required by an organization and skills available in its existing workforce creates a pressing need for new hires. The corollary difficulty in recruiting someone with the needed skills is assessing the real capabilities of the applicant. Despite what the person's résumé says, it's easy to make mistakes in ascertaining someone's readiness for the job at hand. Many analysts point toward a general inequity between what workers bring to a job and what employers need. Economists refer to this inequity as an "imbalance between supply and demand in human resources."

Loyalty and Commitment

Another challenge in getting the right complement of people for an organization is the highs and lows of loyalty and commitment. Employees who feel appreciated and have meaningful work to perform are inclined to be loyal for as long as they are there. But few people feel an obligation to remain once the work ceases to be interesting or if a better opportunity presents itself. Hence the "new loyalty," which is what I call commitment associated with the here and now: Be true to your job and employer for as long as you're there—whether it's for a matter of months or years.

Loyalty works two ways: If employers want it, they have to give it. As a manager, your ability to relate to the expectations of both employee and employer will equip you to spot the deficits in your organization's loyalty profile.

When it comes to loyalty, employees reportedly want their employers to:

➜ Exhibit care and concern in matters of career development and the need for work-family balance.

➜ Offer support and encouragement.

➜ Pay fair and equitable compensation.

➜ Provide fair and equitable workplace policies.

When it comes to loyalty, employers reportedly want their employees to:

➜ Abide by noncompete agreements.

➜ Adhere to company policies and procedures.

➜ Commit to a reasonable length of service.

➜ Speak favorably of them to others.

Outsourcing

One trend that links to fluctuations in the economy and locating people with the right skills is outsourcing. More and more businesses are outsourcing work to individuals in other countries. Depending on where you live, outsourcing means either good fortune or the erosion of opportunities. Outsourcing has left a number of U.S. workers displaced and unemployed, whereas countries such as India have benefited a great deal. The United States Department of Labor, in conjunction with Forrester Research, forecasts an increase in offshore jobs from approximately 588,000 jobs in 2005 to more than 3.3 million jobs in 2015. The job categories, broadly, include management, business, computer, architecture, life sciences, legal, art design, sales, and office jobs.

According to Graham S. Toft, a senior fellow and director of the Center for Economic Competitiveness at the Hudson Institute in Indianapolis, this increase in offshore outsourcing is primarily because education abroad has improved and companies are facing pricing pressures as a result of an increasingly competitive global market.

For many organizations, outsourcing may seem like a sound move to achieve cost savings, to capitalize on time zone differences, and to go where the customers are, but there are drawbacks. In terms of national side effects, there is a loss of high-paying jobs and technical knowledge to workers in foreign countries. In the context of an organization, there is a high potential for a negative impact on employee productivity and morale.

Personnel Expectations

The final one of the considerations related to the need for, and challenges of, making staffing changes hinges on the expectations of workers. The traits I'm going to describe here are generalities and certainly do not apply to everyone, which is extremely important to keep in mind, since those who are exceptions to the "rule" will likely be the first people who come to mind when you begin reviewing the lists. Nonetheless, the following lists provide guidance on factors you want to take into account in relating to your current direct reports and hiring new ones. You will see the topic of generational characteristics resurface in Chapter 6, in relation to leadership behaviors, with the focus there on values of the different groups.

Mature workers (born before 1946) expect a workplace that:

- → Allows for the opportunity to socialize
- → Applies policies, procedures, and performance expectations uniformly and consistently
- → Encourages standardized work ethics
- → Exhibits mutual respect
- → Has a focused corporate vision

→ Maintains a methodical business approach

→ Offers job security

→ Recognizes and rewards loyalty and commitment

→ Sets forth predictable outcomes

→ Values experience

It's easy to think, "All of those people have retired." Many of them have, but they have not disappeared from the workforce, nor have they ceased to exercise influence on workplace dynamics through leadership positions on boards, for example. Their expectations still influence the character of many work environments.

Baby boomers (born between 1946 and 1964) expect a workplace that:

→ Allows work schedule flexibility

→ Applies policies, procedures, and performance expectations uniformly and consistently

→ Emphasizes teamwork

→ Encourages individual workers to make an impact

→ Makes known desirable work ethics

→ Offers a cordial, nonconfrontational environment

→ Publicly recognizes an employee's work

→ Rewards individuals who put in long hours

→ Values new ideas

Again, new managers may think that boomers have waning influence because they either have reached or are about to reach retirement age. Their prospects for longevity, as well as their desire to remain productive and intellectually challenged, continue to make them a significant force in the workplace.

Generation X employees (born between 1964 and 1982) expect a workplace that:

→ Accepts a casual regard for authority

→ Allows for and encourages independence

→ Focuses on outcome rather than task

→ Places little value on policies

→ Provides the latest equipment and technology

→ Supports and encourages work-personal life balance

→ Values and readily offers training and development opportunities

Millennials (born after 1980) expect a workplace that:

→ Provides the latest equipment and technology

→ Incorporates fun

→ Is diverse

→ Strives to make a difference

→ Consistently applies policies, procedures, and expectations

→ Is characterized as being positive and optimistic

→ Encourages individual workers to make an impact

In building a multigenerational workforce, consider the many ways that these different sets of values intersect and can operate in a real-world situation. For example, mature workers, boomers, and millennials all seem to value the application of policies, procedures, and performance expectations uniformly and consistently. Gen Xers have a reputation for placing little value on policies, but you can easily see an individual Gen Xer would have a change of heart if he felt he were being singled out and somehow disadvantaged by a policy.

Similarly, in the arena of relating to fellow workers, mature workers emphasize respect and boomers emphasize teamwork. But with respect comes the ability to be a solid teammate, and with the desire to become a good teammate comes the need to respect. Into that mix, put the millennials' penchant for fun and appreciation of diversity, and once again, it's easy to see the foundation for teamwork and respect. And the Gen X drive for work life-personal life balance again reflects a value that has respect at its core.

THE HIRING PROCESS—RECRUITING

With these common expectations in mind, the next step is designing a plan for recruitment. Before embarking on a recruitment campaign, consider five important factors:

1. *How much money is available.* Factor in the costs of luring the right employee, as well as the cost of finding that person. You may have fixed overhead recruiting expenses and sourcing expenses attached to specific resources such as advertising, but the additional costs could involve relocation expenses and signing bonuses.

2. *How quickly the opening must be filled.* Openings can occur suddenly and unexpectedly, usually when employees decide to leave with little or no advance notice. Anticipation is your best defense. Here are some time-effective methods:

- Keep your employee data bank up-to-date so that you can turn to existing staff members as an immediate resource, even if it's as an interim replacement.

64

- Have an employee referral program in place, and launch it as soon as you know there's an opening.

- Focus on recruitment sources most likely to yield immediate results, such as going through your HR files to identify applicants who were previously interviewed and assessed.

- Turn to your preemployment training pool, if you have one; consider developing one if you do not.

- Hire contingency workers as a stopgap measure.

3. *How wide an audience you'll have to reach to fill the position.* Two primary instances will drive your need to conduct broad-based recruiting: when a position is highly specialized and therefore more challenging to fill, and when you're uncertain as to those qualities that will yield the ideal candidate. Broad-based recruitment sources include employment agencies, search firms, and newspapers. Keep in mind that newspapers available on the Internet potentially reach an audience that goes well beyond your region.

4. *The exemption level of the available position.* The Fair Labor Standards Act defines exempt employees as workers who are legally excluded from receiving overtime compensation. The term *nonexempt* refers to workers who are entitled by law to receive overtime pay. Recruitment sources that produce qualified exempt or professional applicants may not work as well for nonexempt applicants. For example, direct mail recruitment, search firms, and campus recruiting are more likely to produce qualified exempt applicants. High school guidance counselors, government agencies, and employment agencies are more likely to yield a choice group of nonexempt applicants.

5. *What sources for job openings appeal to certain groups.* Knowing what sources are likely to be visited by certain groups can help recruiters narrow their search, but this differentiation gets murkier by the day. For example, millennial applicants (born after 1980) tend to gravitate to interactive and alternative media such as job boards, Internet banner ads, networking sites, e-mail marketing, streaming video, and flash e-cards. At the same time, an increasing number of older candidates have become adept at using social networking sites and Internet-based search tools to locate job opportunities. The nature of the ad or notice itself may do more to help recruit the appropriate candidate than the source of the ad.

Depending on your human and financial resources, consider how you as a manager, and your organization as a whole, might go about both proactive and reactive recruitment.

Being reactive means limiting a recruiter's involvement in the recruitment process. Basically, you wait for applicants to come to you. Popular *reactive recruitment* sources include advertising (e.g., in print), employee referrals, employment agencies and search firms, government agencies, job postings, and radio and television advertising.

Being proactive means active involvement in the recruitment process. You use sources that are more likely to provide recruiters with a direct path to the most suitable applicants. Popular *proactive recruitment* sources include use of social and professional networks, campus recruiting, direct mail, former applicants, job fairs, open houses, military recruiting, and professional associations.

Let's take a closer look at some of these traditional recruitment sources (thirteen in all) and the relative advantages of each. Consider how you, as a manager, may not be the one orchestrating the recruitment activity, but if you're trying to hire a new direct report, your input on style and message in the recruitment effort plays an important role.

1. *Advertising.* Whether in newspapers or professional publications and their companion websites, advertising remains one of the most popular and effective means for soliciting applications. Careful planning in terms of content, timing, and location is likely to generate a large response and result in hiring. Design your advertisement to be one that job hunters want to apply to immediately by using language that creates an image of how great employment with your company would be. Keep in mind that any paper or journal carrying the ad that has an online presence may automatically run the ad on its website. For that reason, inserting keywords and phrases that search engines will pick up should be an integral part of content development.

2. *Campus Recruiting.* Students are attracted to companies that enjoy a good reputation, are successful, will look impressive on their résumés, and keep up with technological change. For many jobs, even at a management level, a person's educational credentials may take a backseat to other skills and job-related knowledge not necessarily acquired through formal education.

3. *Employee Referrals.* This method entails "spreading the word" as soon as a position becomes available. Employees, especially those proven to be valuable and reliable, can often lead their company to prime applicants. To maximize the effectiveness of this method, employers offer incentives of varying worth when employees refer qualified applicants who are ultimately hired and satisfactorily complete a predetermined period of employment at a certain level of performance.

To whatever extent possible, try to keep office politics out of employee referrals. As an example, consider how Apple's public relations director handled a candidate for the position of public relations manager for Apple's federal division. The candidate had been recommended by a senior member of the company's marketing team, who was a personal friend of the candidate. Because of her role as director of communications for a trade association in which Apple participated, the candidate also had a good working relationship with the company's chief lobbyist and a corporate vice president. The PR director showed receptivity to the recommendation, asked once for comments from the other two contacts within the company, and then kept all of the screening and decision making within the appropriate team. By the time she offered the candidate the job, no one could have accused the PR director of pandering to politics. Most important, her handling of the hiring process set the candidate up for success rather than resentment from others on the team, which could have arisen if the hiring were seemingly driven by nepotism.

4. *Online Social Networks and Job Sites.* LinkedIn, Facebook, and other networks hosting groups of people with common interests provide an efficient way to disseminate information about an opportunity. A distinct advantage over other recruitment sources is the ability to reach a global labor pool. Another option is job sites such as Monster.com.

5. *Employment Agencies and Search Firms.* Employment agencies generally recruit for nonexempt and some exempt jobs, while search firms typically handle only professional openings, based on a minimum dollar figure. These recruitment sources have access to a large labor pool and can readily scout the market for qualified applicants.

6. *Former Applicants.* Previously rejected applicants may very well become excellent future employees. Often, there are several qualified applicants for one opening; choosing one does not render the others unqualified.

7. *Government Agencies.* Government agencies are particularly helpful for entry-level and other nonexempt openings. Many organizations, like welfare-to-work agencies and local nonprofits such as those serving individuals with disabilities, provide basic life skills and job training to their clients. In addition, they often offer English as a second language (ESL) training and help those who didn't graduate from high school acquire a general equivalency diploma (GED).

8. *Job Fairs.* Job fairs allow recruiters to interview several applicants over a short period of time, usually one to two days. The fairs are often for a specialized field such as engineering, or they may focus on placing members of specific groups, like women, minorities, or people with disabilities.

9. *Job Postings.* Job posting is a process of internal recruitment whereby available positions are offered to existing staff before exploring outside sources. This process usually creates openings at a lower, easier-to-fill level and saves considerable time and money by transferring someone already familiar with the organizational structure and methodology. It also boosts employee morale.

10. *Military.* Military personnel frequently have a great deal of hands-on experience with a variety of tasks. They tend to have a strong work ethic and understand organizational structure. Other advantages include a background of providing support, both up and down the chain of command, and prior training in teaming as well as managing.

11. *Open Houses.* Organizations that host open houses generally run ads stretching across several geographic locations, as well as post notices on the company website. These ads announce a recruitment drive for specific dates. Unless the company is well known, detailed descriptions of the company's product, reputation, and benefit packages are included. All available jobs with starting salaries or salary ranges are listed as well.

12. *Professional Associations.* Most employers agree that a primary benefit of joining a professional association is the opportunity to network with colleagues from other organizations. It is a good way to find candidates already familiar with your industry if the group is a trade association, and a good way to find certain types of talent, such as graphic designers or software engineers, if the group brings together individual professionals.

13. *Radio and Television.* Radio or television advertising can reach a large audience in a short period of time and tempt prospects not actually looking for a job. This option can be a real plus when you have hard-to-fill positions.

In addition to these traditional means, you can get creative and recruit in malls, advertise on a billboard, throw a party, or do any number of things to attract attention to the opportunities in your organization.

Many of the aforementioned means will simply alert candidates that jobs of a certain kind exist in your organization. Their next step will be to go to your website and search for a complete description and, possibly, an application.

To make that process work smoothly, be sure visitors can navigate the site easily and find the part of the site where job descriptions and listings can be found. Offer a résumé builder service or form that routes the data into your e-mail or database. Records retention laws do apply to applications made over the Internet, so be sure to check on the latest version of the requirement in setting up your application-acceptance system. You also want features that offer a clear picture of your organization's culture. Other guidelines:

➤ *Be prepared to respond to applicants quickly.* After applying for a position within only minutes, candidates will expect a quick response. An auto-response provides instant acknowledgment that material reached its intended destination, but it should indicate a time frame wherein the applicant will receive feedback from a human being.

➤ *Screen out unqualified candidates.* A candidate profiler can help here. Before applicants apply for a job opening, they answer a series of questions designed to determine their qualifications and compatibility with your corporate culture. After reviewing the results, they can decide whether to proceed with an application. The result: a prescreened, interested, and qualified applicant pool. There are myriad potential problems with this approach, unfortunately. If the questions allow lots of room for interpretation, or the candidate profiler brings too many biases or misconceptions to the process, then truly qualified and compatible candidates might be pushed aside.

→ *Take advantage of all the information you can learn about your Web visitors.* You will not hire every applicant expressing an interest in your department or your company, but you can collect data about them that may prove useful to recruitment strategies later on. For example, it may be helpful to ascertain information about the schools or organizations visitors to your website attended or what other pages they've viewed.

You have your candidates. Now what do you do with them?

Before any interviewing begins, be sure both you and the applicant have the same job description in front of you. Review it thoroughly to become thoroughly familiar with the qualities being sought. You want to be sure these qualities are job-related and realistic and that they communicate the duties of the available position clearly. You also want to be prepared to provide additional information to applicants.

Guidelines for Writing Effective Job Descriptions

→ Arrange duties and responsibilities in a logical, sequential order.

→ State separate duties clearly and concisely.

→ Identify "essential" and "nonessential" functions of the job.

→ Identify an approximate percentage of time needed to perform each task.

→ Avoid generalizations or ambiguous words.

→ Do not try to list every task.

→ Include specific examples of duties.

➤ Use nontechnical language, unless technical language is inherent to the job.

➤ Avoid referring to specific people.

➤ Use the present tense.

➤ Be objective and accurate in describing the job.

➤ Use "action words"—that is, words that describe a specific function, such as "organizes."

➤ Stress what the incumbent does, instead of attempting to explain a procedure that must be used. (For example, state clearly that the person in this position "records appointments" instead of saying "a record of appointments must be kept.")

➤ Ensure that all requirements are job-related and in accordance with applicable Equal Employment Opportunity (EEO) laws.

Finally, have a schedule for reviewing job descriptions of your direct reports—do it at least once a year—to be sure that the jobs match the organization's needs.

THE HIRING PROCESS—INTERVIEWING

Before the interview begins, review the candidate's résumé or application to be sure that the person's qualifications match the job requirements on the job description. The review will also give you a chance to identify holes and anomalies in the résumé that invite questions, such as jobs that overlap in time or gaps in employment or work history. In addition to those red flags, others would include apparent inconsistencies between education and experience, frequency of job changes, confusing job titles, and irregular salary history.

Applicants must feel comfortable with the interview environment if they are to provide information regarding their work history and qualifications, so ensure privacy and try to avert interruptions. Have every-thing you will need ready before the applicant arrives, including the application, résumé, job description, and any other related documents such as an organizational chart and benefits information. And consider both distance and the presence of barriers in the interview environment. Ideally, the applicant should sit four to five feet from you and not on the other side of a huge desk, and the person shouldn't be shielded from you by your laptop screen, either. Rapport building is integral to the inter-view, so in addition to setting up the room in a way that supports good rapport, ask questions at the outset to promote it. They would include icebreaker questions such as "Did you have any trouble getting here?" and "How were the directions we provided?"

To begin the actual job interview, be ready to do the following:

→ Identify information on the completed application and/or résumé requiring elaboration or clarification.

→ Review the job description, identifying required skills and expe-rience, and develop questions that will determine whether the applicant meets these standards.

→ Ask about a half-dozen prepared questions that are broad enough so that the applicant's responses will trigger additional questions. They would include questions such as these:

- Please describe your activities during a typical day at your (present/most recent) job.

- What do/did you like most and least about your (present/most recent) job?

- Describe a situation in your (present/most recent) job involving _____. How did you handle it?

- What are/were some of the duties in your (present/most recent) job that you find/found to be particularly difficult or easy?

- How do you generally approach tasks you dislike? Give me a specific example from your (present/most recent) job.

- What has prepared you for this job?

If the person has no prior work experience, ask about favorite subjects, study habits, and approaches to handling deadlines; also pose the question about what prepared the candidate for this particular job. In fact, regardless of the applicant's educational or work background, that last question should always be included. For some positions, a type of role-playing might also illuminate the candidate's qualifications. For example, you might pose a situation in which a customer asks a particular question and ask the candidate, "How would you handle that?"

There are really only five effective employment interview questioning techniques: competency (general and job-specific), open-ended, hypothetical, probing, and closed-ended questioning. Here is a summary of what each technique covers.

General Competency

A *competency* is defined as a skill, trait, quality, or characteristic that contributes to a person's ability to effectively perform the duties and responsibilities of a job. Competencies are the gauges for job success. Identifying job-specific competencies enables you to assess how effective a person has been in the past and, therefore, how effectively she is likely to perform in your organization.

While every job requires different competencies, there are four primary categories:

1. Tangible or measurable skills

2. Knowledge

3. Behavior

4. Interpersonal skills

Most jobs emphasize the need for one category over the others, but every employee should be able to demonstrate competencies, to some extent, in all four categories.

Tangible or Measurable Skills

Tangible competencies demonstrate what applicants have done in past jobs. For example, competencies for a technical job could include having overall technical know-how, being able to tailor technical information to different audiences, applying technical expertise to solve business problems, staying technologically current, understanding the technologies of the organization, optimizing technology, balancing multiple projects, and communicating project status.

Knowledge

The second competency—knowledge—concerns what applicants know and how they think. Included in this category are project management skills, problem-solving abilities, decision-making skills, the ability to focus on key elements of a project, time management, and the effective use of resources. These are considered intangible qualities—more difficult to measure and quantify than concrete skills, but no less important. Every job, regardless of level, requires a certain degree of knowledge. Even an entry-level position demands some degree of decision making or problem solving. Interviewers should ask knowledge-related questions appropriate to the level and nature of the job to determine not only what applicants know, but also how they think. This is especially important when jobs don't require previous measurable experience, thereby precluding the ability to draw from past job-related experiences.

Behavior

The third competency concerns how an applicant acts under certain conditions. Suppose the position calls for a high level of client satisfaction. In past client-oriented jobs, were the applicants committed to developing lasting partnerships with clients? Did they keep clients informed of key developments and follow up to ensure client satisfaction? There are numerous questions you can ask applicants with regard to job-specific behaviors that will reveal whether they will function effectively in the company's environment.

Interpersonal Skills

The fourth and final competency involves interpersonal skills—that is, how applicants interact with others. Do they actively listen? Can they exercise self-control when upset? Are they self-motivated and able to work effectively with a wide range of people? Do they respect the views and ideas of others? Are they receptive to feedback? Can they manage conflict effectively?

Every job requires some degree of interaction with others. Regardless of how competent they may be at what they can do, what they know, and how they behave, if individuals are unable to interact effectively with their managers, coworkers, employees, or clients, then their work and the work of others will suffer.

Job-Specific Competency

Each job requires competencies from all four categories—tangible skills, knowledge, behavior, and interpersonal skills. Once you've acquired information about the job, then isolate *job-specific competencies.* This is a two-step procedure: 1) Make a list of all the required job-specific competencies, and 2) identify each competency according to its category—tangible skill, knowledge, behavior, or interpersonal skill. You will no doubt see a greater emphasis on some competencies than on others. Often, competencies are paired. Tangible skills and knowledge generally fall together, as do behaviors and interpersonal skills.

At the end of the interview, you will need to go for the close. Even though it's only about 5 percent of the interview in terms of time, this phase involves questions that could have tremendous weight in your decision making. Sample closing-stage questions include:

"What additional examples of your work with difficult customers would help me make a hiring decision in your favor?"

"What else can you tell me about your dealings with Six Sigma that will help me understand your expertise in this area?"

"What additional examples of your knowledge and/or expertise can you offer in support of your candidacy for this position?"

Because of laws and regulations affecting workers, be careful to avoid certain questions. Here are two simple rules:

1. Avoid questions that are not job-related.

2. Avoid receiving non-job-related information. Interviewers may be found guilty of discrimination if an applicant volunteers illegal information and such information is used in making a hiring decision.

Questions to Determine Competency

➔ Competency questions should focus on relating past job performance to probable future on-the-job behavior. The questions are based on information relevant to specific job-related skills, abilities, and traits. The answers reveal the likelihood of similar future performance.

➔ Their design helps you seek specific examples. These examples allow you to project how an applicant is likely to perform in your organization.

➔ They begin with a lead-in phrase that alerts the applicant to the fact that you want specific examples. Here are three examples of competency question lead-ins:

  • Describe a time when you ...

- Give an example of a time when you ...

- Tell me about a specific job experience in which you ...

→ They are legally defensible.

→ They should represent about 70 percent of an interview, supplemented by other types of questions.

Competency-based interviews allow you to make hiring decisions based on facts. They improve the interview by helping you to identify the skills and characteristics needed to succeed in a specific work environment and to clarify what applicants have learned from their experiences and how they might apply what they have learned to the job at hand. Through an exploration of candidates' competencies, you also learn how they acquired them.

The other four questioning styles described previously in Chapter 1, in the section on Effective Communication—open-ended, closed-ended, probing, and hypothetical questions—all have a place in the interview process. They are tools to discover applicants' competencies, both general and job-specific.

Following are advantages, cautions, and examples of these questions in the context of a job interview:

Open-Ended Questions

→ *Advantages:* They invite conversation, which gives you a chance to ascertain a person's communications skills as well as facts about the applicant. They are also helpful in interviewing shy applicants because they remove the pressure that can accompany a competency-based question requiring the recollection of specific examples.

→ *Cautions:* Open-ended questions can sometimes result in descriptive monologues lacking substance or verifiable information. In addition, some open-ended questions are too broad in scope, such as the classic, "Tell me about yourself." A more specific version of that question establishes useful boundaries while still being open-ended: "Please describe your work experience over the past three years."

➤ *Examples:*

- What is your description of the ideal manager? Work environment? Work schedule?

- How would you describe yourself as an employee? Co-worker? Manager?

- What kind of people do you find it difficult/easy to work with? Why?

- What do you feel an employer owes an employee? How about what an employee owes an employer?

- What were some of the duties of your last job that you found to be difficult? What made them difficult? What about duties that you found to be easy? What made them easy?

- How do you feel about the progress that you have made in your career to date? Where are you career-wise in terms of where you thought you'd be five years ago?

- How did your last job differ from the one you had before it? Which one was preferable? Why?

- In what ways do you feel your present job has prepared you to assume additional responsibilities?

- What does the prospect of this job offer you that your last job did not?

- What immediate and long-term goals have you set for yourself?

Closed-Ended Questions

➔ *Advantages*: They give interviewers an added measure of control, put nervous applicants at ease, provide greater clarification, and yield concise answers. And if there is a single issue that could terminate the interview, such as the absence of an important job requirement, asking about it up front in a direct, closed-ended way can disclose what you need to know quickly and succinctly.

➔ *Cautions*: Too many closed-ended questions provide limited information, resulting in an incomplete picture of the person's abilities and experiences and rendering you unable to assess the applicant's verbal communication skills, if relevant.

➔ *Examples*:

- How often do you travel for your current job?

- Are you aware that the starting salary for this job is $_____?

- Based on what you have told me so far, can I assume that you prefer working independently rather than as part of a team?

- How many times did you step in for your manager in the last three months?

- Earlier you said that the most challenging part of your job is conducting new-hire orientations. Just before, you indicated that you favor conducting interviews. Please clarify.

Probing Questions

➔ *Advantages*: They enable interviewers to delve more deeply for additional information. Applicants who have trouble providing full answers usually appreciate the extra help that comes from a probing question. These questions also show applicants that you're interested in what they are saying and want to learn more.

→ *Cautions*: Allowing probing questions to be the dominant style can put applicants on the defensive.

→ *Examples*:

- What kind of people do you find it difficult/easy to work with? Why?

- Do you take over for your manager when your manager is away? How often?

- What motivates you? Why?

- Who or what has influenced you with regard to your career goals? In what way?

- You said earlier that your team failed to meet the last deadline. What do you believe caused that to happen?

- What are some of the problems you encountered in your last job? How did you resolve them?

- What would your coworkers say about your contributions to the last team project you participated in?

Hypothetical Questions

→ *Advantages*: They allow for the evaluation of reasoning abilities, thought processes, values, attitudes, creativity, work style, and approach to different tasks. Hypothetical questions are appropriate for applicants with limited or no work experience; they are also helpful in interviews for jobs with little or no tangible requirements.

→ *Cautions*: Although the answers to hypothetical questions can produce important information about the applicant's reasoning ability and thought processes, interviewers are cautioned against expecting correct answers. Without familiarity with the organization, applicants can offer responses based only on their previous experiences. Such answers, then, are based on how they think rather than what they know.

➡ *Examples*:

- How would you handle an employee who is consistently tardy?

- How would you handle a long-term employee whose performance has always been outstanding, but who recently started to make a number of mistakes in her work?

- What would you say to an employee who challenged your authority?

- Consider this scenario: You've just given a presentation and are asked a series of questions to which you do not know the answers. What would you do?

- Suppose you are a member of a team and disagree with the way the others want to approach a project. How would you go about trying to change their minds?

- If you were given a task that created an undue amount of pressure, what would you do?

- How would you avoid conflict with coworkers? Your manager? Clients?

You will put these questions to work in the context of either a screening or a comprehensive interview. Screening interviews are primarily the purview of the human resources professionals, but depending on the size of an organization, screening responsibilities could fall to any manager looking to hire a direct report.

There are three key objectives for conducting screening interviews, which might be conducted face-to-face, over the phone, or using an audio/video link: 1) to establish continued interest on the part of both the interviewer and applicant; 2) to determine preliminary job suitability; and 3) to eliminate from the running applicants who do not meet the minimum requirements of the job and/or in whom you have no further interest.

Here are guidelines on how you might want to use—or not use—the different question types in a screening interview:

- ➔ Determine what the applicant currently does (open-ended) and his current salary (closed-ended).

- ➔ Based on the isolated tasks and job requirements, determine the level and nature of the applicant's expertise by asking a series of six to eight competency-based questions.

- ➔ Wind down with one or two open-ended and/or closed-ended questions to confirm what the applicant has told you.

- ➔ Conclude by asking, "What else should I know about you in relation to your application for this job?"

- ➔ Reserve probing questions; they are rarely introduced in exploratory interviews, unless the applicant's responses to competency-based questions are incomplete.

- ➔ Omit hypotheticals, except when the applicant has no prior work experience to draw upon.

The primary objectives of a comprehensive interview are 1) to identify the applicant likely to be the most suitable match for a job in terms of both tangible and intangible qualities, and 2) to select the person deemed the best overall fit for the organization. If someone from your HR department conducts a comprehensive interview, the questions will likely be somewhat broad and organization-oriented rather than job-specific. Questions you might ask a potential direct report would be more job-specific. For example, let's say you are interviewing someone for the position of business office supervisor. Here's how the line of questioning might proceed:

- → Tell me how you go about organizing the billing for your office. (open-ended)

- → How do you handle receipt errors? (open-ended)

- → Tell me about the worst receipt error you ever had to handle. (competency)

- → Do you handle payment overages? (closed-ended)

- → Describe your logging system. (open-ended)

- → What's your approach to collecting delinquent accounts? (open-ended)

- → Describe an instance when you had a delinquent account open for a really long time. What ultimately happened? (competency)

- → How do you maintain payroll records? (open-ended)

- → Describe your system of financial recordkeeping. (open-ended)

- → What would you say if someone suggested you switch over to another system? (hypothetical)

- → Tell me about a time when you were blamed for a financial error that wasn't your fault. (competency)

- → What would you do if I wasn't around and one of the company's VPs became upset over not having received important financial documents? (hypothetical) Has that ever happened to you? (closed-ended) Tell me about it. (competency)

- → I need someone to revise policies and procedures relevant to the business office function. Have you ever done that? (closed-ended)

➔ How would you go about doing it? (hypothetical) Whom would you talk to? (hypothetical)

➔ What do you consider to be the most important thing when it comes to preparing a financial report? (open-ended)

Another way to conduct comprehensive interviews is with a small team. You can still ask the same kinds of questions as in a one-on-one interview, but the questions come from different people. If carefully planned, team interviews can be highly effective for several reasons. They tend to be more objective because there's more interaction with the applicant by more than one person. While one of the panelists is talking, the other two can more carefully observe the applicant's body language and take additional time to assess responses to specific questions. If there are three different personality types on the panel, you'll be able to see how the applicant responds to and interacts with these different types. Finally, assessments tend to be more accurate and consistent, since everyone is basing decisions on the same information.

To wrap up what happens in a job interview—and how you want to make it flow—consider the components: 1) setting a format whereby you balance asking questions and providing information and 2) practicing active listening, which includes understanding the role of body language.

Interview Format

The format of an interview should incorporate five critical phases:

1. Making introductory remarks about what will happen during the interview. Telling the applicant what's about to take place may seem unnecessary—after all, both parties know it's a job interview. But the way in which this information is conveyed sets the tone for the meeting and alerts the applicant about what to expect over the next hour or so.

2. Asking questions about an applicant's education and prior work history. Questions must relate to the requirements of the job as well as other relevant but intangible categories.

3. Providing information about the job opening, its salary and benefits, and the organization.

4. Answering questions about the job and the organization.

5. Informing the applicant what happens next before ending the interview on a positive note.

Just as some interviewers have trouble knowing how to begin interviews, others are uncertain about how to end them. To help you decide if it's time to close an interview, ask yourself the following questions:

➡ Have I asked the applicant enough questions about her education and previous experience to determine job suitability?

➡ Have I adequately described the available position and provided sufficient information about this organization?

➡ Have I discussed salary, benefits, growth opportunities, and other related topics to the extent that the policy of this company permits?

➡ Have I allowed the applicant to ask questions?

If you have a high level of interest in an applicant, the closing will involve committing to a subsequent interview. Candidates in whom you have a moderate or low interest should get a "thank you" and be informed that someone from the company will contact them. In the case of a person of no interest to you, be sure that contact occurs promptly, so the individual can get on with the job search.

The order in which interviewers cover these five phases is largely a matter of preference with the exception of the first and last phases—obviously telling the applicant what's going to take place during the interview has to occur at the outset, and informing the applicant of what will happen after the interview needs to take place at the end. Any order you select for phases two, three, and four will work, as long as it reflects your own personality and style. If you feel comfortable, the applicant is likely to respond well to whatever format you select.

Active Listening

Many interviewers talk too much, erroneously believing that they're more in control of the interview as long as they're talking. No more than 25 percent of your time should be devoted to talking. This time should be spent asking questions about the applicant's qualifications, clarifying points, providing information about the job and the organization, and answering job- and organization-related questions. Otherwise, listen actively.

Here are guidelines for active listening:

➡ *Listen for connecting themes and ideas.* By not focusing on every word, you can concentrate on key job-related information.

➡ *Summarize periodically.* Applicants don't always provide complete answers to questions at one time, so you have to fit the pieces together. To make certain that you're accurately getting the full picture, periodically stop and summarize what the applicant is telling you. For example: "Let me make certain that I understand exactly what you've accomplished in this area. You weren't directly responsible for running the department, but your boss was away one-quarter of the time, and during that time you ran the department. Is this correct?" The applicant may then say, "Technically speaking, I didn't run the department. If there were any problems, it was up to me to get in touch with the boss to find out what we should do." This clarifies the scope and extent of the applicant's responsibility.

➔ *Filter out distractions.* Distractions can include other people coming into your office, the phone ringing, and focusing your thoughts elsewhere. By not listening actively, you're likely to miss important information that could influence the final hiring decision.

➔ *Screen out personal biases and emotional influences.* Don't allow personal opinions or a bad mood to interfere with active listening. Generational biases, such as an aversion to a style of clothing or accessories that seem "dated" or "outrageous," can be difficult to get past; focus on the content of responses and behavior as much as possible. The opposite effect can occur, of course—that is, a bias in favor of someone who is very attractive or reminds you of a dear friend. That's as much of a trap as a negative bias.

➔ *Listen with your body.* Occasional nods or smiles in response to the applicant's communication reinforce the fact that you have an interest in what is being said. Keep your body language open, which suggests you want the person to speak. For example, remove barriers such as laptops and phones from the space between you and the applicant, and gesture with open hands.

SELECTION GUIDELINES

Regardless of your department, hiring a direct report involves you in at least three of the five major steps in bringing on any new employee. All five are listed here because your involvement in some processes, such as conducting background checks and testing, may either overlap with activities of the HR department or you may have HR-related responsibilities as part of your job description.

Step 1: Overview

→ Review your objectives.

→ Review the job description for the duties and responsibilities of the position, as well as other required tangible skills and knowledge.

→ Consider the intangible requirements of the job.

→ Consider your company's affirmative action goals.

Step 2: The Interview

→ Review and compare multiple applicants' reactions to various questions.

→ Consider each applicant's nonverbal communication patterns.

→ Consider the salary requirements of each candidate in relation to the salary range for the position.

→ Review each applicant's reasons for leaving previous employers.

→ Assess each applicant's potential.

Step 3: References and Background Checks

→ Weigh the implications of checking references—that is, weigh the risk of charges of defamation of character against charges of negligent hiring and retention that may stem from not checking references.

→ Consider information acquired from the Internet, telephone reference checks, and educational institutions.

→ Factor in relevant information acquired as a result of background checks.

Step 4: Testing

→ Identify the relationship of a test to a person's likely ability to successfully perform the essentials of a job.

→ Determine how heavily test results should weigh in making a final decision.

Step 5: Selection

→ Balance input received as a result of the interview with the results of reference checks and tests.

→ Consider who will be the best fit overall for the job, within the department, and in the organization.

A final, general thought might be to hire with the big picture in mind. Every organization has projects, with some of them carrying considerable weight in terms of short- or long-term success. However, hiring for a project, with the idea that the individual will settle into the ongoing work of the organization later, has the potential to create problems for the individual, the manager, and the entire organization. Keep this in mind while reading the next chapter on project management—that all projects should have clear alignment with big-picture organizational priorities, and that your hires should be people who can help in more ways than one toward those priorities.

CHAPTER 4

Managing Projects

Project management means people management. That is the central notion to keep in mind. You have to stay alert for red flags concerning money and deadlines, of course, but unless you apply your skills managing human resources, your ability to manage things has limited value to the project.

How an organization differentiates between a project and a task is based on the organization itself. Producing trade-show collateral could be a task for the marketing department of a large company that participates in a dozen trade shows a year, whereas a small company that exhibits at one show a year might deem it a project.

The standard definition of a project is that it is "a temporary endeavor undertaken to create a unique product, service, or result." This definition, and a number of others referenced in this chapter, come from the Project Management Institute (PMI) and its fourth edition of *A Guide to the Project Management Body of Knowledge* (simply known as the *PMBOK Guide*). The *PMBOK Guide* is a standard for project management, and if you will be faced with the management of large projects, you will want to become familiar with the standard. Experts in the standard can earn the credential of Project Management Professional (PMP) from PMI.

THE TRIPLE CONSTRAINTS

A project generally has an established budget, time frame, and scale, unlike a task, for which funding or deadlines may be open-ended. In short, time, cost, and scope are often referred to as the triple constraints of a project. A constraint is the state, quality, or sense of being restricted to a given course of action. Simply put, it is anything that limits your flexibility when managing the project.

The Project Triangle

Scope
Requirements

However, time, cost, and scope are not the only considerations. The project manager must also consider:

➤ Risk

➤ Resources

➤ Quality

If one or more of these factors changes, the project manager (PM) considers the impact on the other factors. So the simplest way to define project management is the balancing of six factors—time, cost, scope, risk, resources, and quality. For example, if the customer requests early delivery, additional resources might have to be added, which will increase the costs. If costs cannot be increased due to budget limitations, then maybe the scope (requirements) of the project needs to be reduced. The project team members assist the project manager with the assessment, keeping the focus on delivering a successful project.

There are many ways to view the triple constraints—and one of them is to not necessarily see them as constraints. A classic example of this different perspective came out of the construction project to rebuild the Santa Monica Freeway after the Northridge earthquake of January 17, 1994. Earthquake damage caused a complete closure of the freeway, known as the busiest in America and the main East-West route to downtown Los Angeles. Companies threatened to move, tax revenue was down, and there was the real possibility of a ripple effect resulting in a regional depression.

With that threat looming, the city set a goal to get the freeway up and running again in an absurdly small amount of time. City officials issued the request for a bid and then managed the contract. They were not construction experts, but they did have money and the immediate need for a rebuilt freeway.

The city officials were willing to pay dearly for speed—and to penalize for any loss of speed—so money was not a constraint; it was an incentive. The contracting company, C. C. Myers, Inc., posts on its website the following description of the challenge, and the highly successful way the contractor met that challenge:

Contract requirements allowed a maximum completion time of 140 calendar days with a penalty for late completion of $205,000 per calendar day and an incentive of $200,000 per day for early completion. Contract time commenced on Saturday, the 5th of February, with materials and equipment moving to the jobsite that day and through the weekend. Even though the final construction plans were not available until February 26th, C. C. Myers, Inc. immediately went to work on a 24-hour-day, 7-days-per-week schedule with up to 400 workmen on the job, while maintaining a [sterling] safety record.

Sixty-six days after the contract was signed the freeway was opened to traffic, 74 days ahead of schedule. The opening of the Santa Monica Freeway allowed over 350,000 vehicles a day to once again move between downtown Los Angeles and the Santa Monica area. This effort saved costs calculated at over one million dollars to the public for each day the freeway was shut down.

THE PROJECT TEAM

Picture the project manager as the coach and other people assigned to work on the project as the team. Accomplishing the project takes the entire team, with everyone working together toward a shared goal, to get the job done.

Each team member needs defined roles and responsibilities for the project and project work. The project team, under the direction of the project manager, defines what needs to be done to execute the project, and then specific assignments are handed to team members.

Typical roles of project team members include:

→ Project sponsor

→ Project manager

→ Project management team member (who performs project man-agement–related functions, such as maintaining the schedule)

→ Team members (usually subject matter experts, or SMEs, and those who perform product work)

→ Team leaders (person with the most tenure when multiple peo-ple assigned)

PROJECT FLOW

View projects in terms of both phases and processes. Phases describe elements of the project life cycle, whereas processes are the actions occurring within the phases to accomplish the project. In general terms, the phases of a project can be captured as follows:

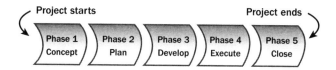

As a general rule, an end-of-phase review meeting is held at the end of each phase to review progress, work done, and deliverables, as well as to decide whether to carry on with the project, change it, put it on hold, or cancel it.

Although the types of processes have names similar to those commonly used for the phases of a project, processes differ in that they are repeatable. Think of them in these terms:

1. *Initiating*, or the process of authorizing or starting the project, which involves developing specific types of documentation

2. *Planning*, which entails defining what has to be done and tactics for doing it (i.e., planning the work)

3. *Executing*, or doing the work identified and producing deliverables (i.e., working the plan)

4. *Monitoring and controlling*, which entails tracking the project, reviewing progress, identifying variances, and taking corrective actions

5. *Closing*, or the process for formally concluding the project, which entails the preparation of checklists and the assembly of all paperwork, as well as other tasks

Here is a step-by-step look at the project flow:

→ The project starts with the creation and approval of the project charter.

→ The project manager and the team plan the project work.

→ The scope statement takes shape.

→ The work breakdown structure and the activities list are built.

→ Estimates are generated for time, resources, and costs.

→ The project schedule comes together.

→ Work is done according to the plan.

→ Reports are generated.

→ Meetings occur.

→ Changes are controlled.

→ Project deliverables are turned over to the appropriate stakeholder.

→ The project ends.

DIFFERENTIATING OPERATIONS FROM PROJECTS

While business requests and orders serve to trigger operations, ideas and new requirements lead to projects. Operations are routine activities that sustain the organization and its infrastructure over time. This routine work doesn't end when current objectives are met; instead, the work follows new directions to sustain the organization.

Projects often differ from operations simply because they produce change.

Project work is work that begins and ends within a specified time frame and produces something new. Projects can originate from any department—engineering, finance, marketing, sales, help desk, customer service, IT support, or administration.

Projects can include product launches or advertising campaigns, trade-show exhibits, packaging changes, office relocations, and organization restructuring. Projects also arise from the need to comply with newly introduced industry standards or government regulations.

Since projects cause or result in change once they are deployed or delivered to customers, the keys to managing successful projects can be summarized in two statements:

→ Every project must align with something bigger than itself.

→ Every project should link to an organizational goal, objective, or strategy.

At the outset, you need to be able to recognize the value of the project to the organization and to yourself. Part of that action is the ability to explain the elements of a project charter, and its relevance to initiating a project, and to identify stakeholders and their roles on a project.

INITIATING A PROJECT

Step one in moving forward with a project is ensuring that it aligns with organizational priorities. You want to create a project charter to specify how that alignment occurs as it relates to:

→ Business goals and objectives

→ Business strategies and timetables

→ Corporate culture, core values, and beliefs

→ Organizational structure

→ Operating policies, practices, procedures, and business systems

Besides providing a general overview of the project, the charter formally authorizes the project, identifies the project manager, and provides the project manager with the authority to manage the project. Normally, the project sponsor, initiator, or some other senior person in the organization creates the charter, although sometimes the project manager participates in its creation, too. Whether the charter is written with or without your involvement, it is important to understand what goes into the project charter because you may need to use it as a source for other project documentation you will be involved in creating.

The document should address the following elements:

➤ Purpose or justification of the project

➤ Project objectives and success criteria

➤ High-level requirements

➤ High-level project description

➤ Characteristics of the product

➤ Assigned project manager and this manager's responsibility/ authority level

➤ Summary budget

➤ Summary milestone schedule

➤ Approval requirements

➤ Name and responsibility of the person authorizing the project charter

A template is supplied here to use as a model for developing a project charter; it is followed by a completed template example.

TEMPLATE FOR CREATING A PROJECT CHARTER

PROJECT CHARTER

Insert your project name.

BUSINESS CASE

Problem/Opportunity:
Insert a brief description of the problem or opportunity driving the project.

Projected Solution:
Insert a brief description of the solution you envision.

Expected Benefits:
Insert a description of the benefits the project is expected to yield to the department or to the organization as a whole.

Estimated Costs:
Insert personnel costs, on a full-time-employee basis, for some increment of the project's duration, such as per week or per month, as well as estimates of the money needed for the project. Include any significant physical resources the project might require.

PROJECT DESCRIPTION

Insert a short description of the project, including the deliverable(s) that will be created.

Now let's look at a sample project charter that suggests how the template could be completed (in this example, by an organization that develops educational conferences for library professionals).

SAMPLE PROJECT CHARTER

PROJECT CHARTER

National Conference on Digital Media in Libraries

BUSINESS CASE

Problem/Opportunity:
Many library professionals need mentoring in integrating digital media into their libraries and library systems.

Projected Solution:
Approximately 100 library professionals will receive guidance from hands-on experts.

Expected Benefits:
Attendees will be equipped with best practices and specific resources on the integration of digital media at their facilities so that they can immediately begin to improve customer service. Conference organizer will make a profit through registration fees and sponsorships.

Estimated Costs:

❑ *Planning/Personnel*—Equivalent of one full-time administrative staff person for two months and one full-time manager for one month (both spread over a six-month planning period)

SAMPLE PROJECT CHARTER

❏ *Execution/Personnel*—Three full-time administrative staff members for three days and two full-time managers for three days

❏ *Estimated Cost*—$60,000 (Note: Estimated cost expected to be offset by income totaling $64,000.)

PROJECT DESCRIPTION

Speakers from library systems and individual libraries that have led the way in integrating digital media into their facilities will provide best practices, trend information, and other practical guidance to fellow library professionals. The two-and-one-half days of keynotes and panels will equip attendees with information and resources so that they can return to their organizations and immediately begin to improve services to their users. The conference will include a workshop-format session in which attendees will break into groups to create solutions for specific types of problems related to digital media in libraries. If successful, the conference will become an annual event, intended to both aid constituents and earn revenue for our organization.

A short narrative on the project, such as provided in the previous example, is useful for any project, including short-term, narrowly defined projects. For complicated, expensive, and/or long-term projects, you will benefit greatly by creating a detailed analysis.

A detailed analysis identifies project priorities, stakeholders, constraints, assumptions, deliverables, requirements, activities that are outside the scope of the project, budget estimates, schedule estimates, milestones, external elements on which the project is dependent for success, and potential risks associated with the project.

Continuing with the example of the library conference project, the following expanded template will help to organize your thinking about each of the elements needed in a detailed project analysis.

PROJECT PRIORITIES

	Least Flexible	Flexible (2nd)	Most Flexible (3rd)
Scope			
Schedule			
Budget			

Scope Flexibility Range:
Describe the sponsor's acceptable scope range for the project.
If the project sponsor is the director of educational programs, for example, then marketing activities may be outside the scope of the project, even if they seem related. You would want to determine whether you have flexibility on including marketing activities.

Schedule Flexibility Range:
Describe the sponsor's acceptable schedule range for the project.
In military planning, the concept of "no later than" (often abbreviated NLT) helps immediately establish one element of a project schedule. Backplanning from that date gives you an initial cut on the project schedule. In looking at that schedule, if you immediately see that the sponsor's NLT date can only be achieved by starting the project much earlier (e.g., last month) or by adding five people to the project, then the sponsor has what she needs to determine where she can be more flexible with time or with resources.

Budget Flexibility Range:
Describe the sponsor's acceptable budget range for the project.
Budget includes money as well as resources that cost the organization money, such as employees, equipment, and space. For

PROJECT PRIORITIES

example, if your project requires a weekly two-hour meeting to stay on track, then the organization needs to have a space for that meeting.

STAKEHOLDERS

Name	Role	Functional Area	Phone	E-Mail

CONSTRAINTS

ASSUMPTIONS

DELIVERABLES

REQUIREMENTS

Cont'd.

PROJECT PRIORITIES

OUT-OF-SCOPE ACTIVITIES

BUDGET ESTIMATES

Total Full-Time Employees:
Insert initial schedule estimate.
Your project may require employees at different levels within the company, such as a combination of your direct reports and a peer of yours from another department. In making the estimates, note that fact.

Total Expenses:
Insert initial expense estimate.
Again, expenses aren't only funds required for consultants, equipment, or other aspects of the project. If you need to commandeer three PCs dedicated to computer-generated imagery for a month, then that resource must be logged as an expense to the company.

SCHEDULE ESTIMATES

Start Date:
Insert estimated start date.

Completion Date:
Insert estimated completion date.
As referenced previously, the concept of "no later than" as perceived by the project sponsor is a good date to insert here.

PROJECT PRIORITIES

MILESTONES

EXTERNAL DEPENDENCIES

RISKS

The terms used in the project charter template are either self-explanatory or receive attention in the next section, on planning a project. One critical term that is often misunderstood—a confusion that sets a project on a wrong course from the planning stages—is that of "stakeholder."

A *stakeholder* is anyone working on or affected by the project or its product.

Aligning what different stakeholders hope to achieve is critical to project success. Differing needs and interests can impede progress. By knowing the needs of all stakeholders, you can better predict their actions and reactions.

Stakeholders can have different levels of responsibility for a project, authority over it, and extent of interest or activity, depending upon where the project is on the time line. Stakeholders fall into several categories, and typically include the following:

→ **Customers/End-Users.** This group includes persons or organizations that request or require the product of the project and will use it. Customers can be internal, external, or both.

   Example: *In the sample project description, library professionals in need of digital media training would constitute the customers/ end-users.*

→ **Sponsor.** This individual is the source of financial resources; the sponsor might also be the project champion or the person who serves as an interface between the project and senior management.

   Example: *In the case of the library conference, the sponsor is likely the head of the professional association serving the librarians. This is the person who can write the checks for collateral, sign the contracts with the hotel, and assign personnel to the project.*

→ **Project Manager.** The person responsible for achieving project objectives assumes the role of project manager. The project manager is responsible for developing the project plan, executing according to the plan, monitoring and controlling the project, and reporting on the project's progress.

   Example: *In the example given, either a staff person or a consultant can assume the role of project manager. Projects such as conferences, construction jobs, and others that may lie slightly outside the mission and activities of an organization and its staff commonly have a project manager who comes from the outside.*

→ **Project Management Team.** The management team includes the people working on the project who are directly involved in activities, such as performing detailed analysis of project risks or maintaining the project schedule for the project manager.

Example: *The library conference would logically involve the organization's office manager and administrative assistant.*

→ **Project Team.** This team could be staff members or consultants assigned to the project, including the project manager and project management team, who accomplish the work on the project, such as creating detailed design documents or providing time estimates for specific tasks. Subject matter experts (SMEs) often fall into this category.

Example: *The library conference team, for example, could include other consultants with responsibilities for soliciting sponsorship or promoting the event to the target audiences.*

→ **Functional Managers.** Managers of a functional or administrative area of the business who often provide resources or subject matter expertise to the project fit into this group. Programmers, designers, or developers of equipment to produce prototypes are examples.

Example: *The head of educational programs for the group would be a functional manager who would have a place on the team for the library conference project.*

→ **Portfolio Managers.** These people may or may not be staff members. They are high-level managers responsible for establishing the priorities of multiple projects (which may or may not be related), monitoring their progress, and evaluating whether they are adding value to the organization.

Example: *In the case of a not-for-profit organization staging a conference, the portfolio managers would likely be the board of directors or perhaps the organization's steering committee.*

➤ **Program Managers.** Generally speaking, these are managers who oversee and coordinate related projects; the purpose is to achieve benefits and efficiencies not possible were the projects managed individually. Program managers can, for instance, allocate resources from a single pool, based on the priority of a project.

> **Example:** *When consultants are used to manage a project such as a conference, they are chosen often because their experience and connections create certain cost efficiencies that a completely in-house effort might not be able to achieve. If the consultant does six conferences a year at a particular hotel, for example, that could yield advantages to the client company (and the profit objectives for the project).*

➤ **Vendors.** These stakeholders are external to the company in every way. They provide goods and services needed on the project.

> **Example:** *For a conference, the vendors would include the caterer and the company hired to create digital records of sessions.*

Stakeholders might even include government agencies, industry-specific organizations such as trade associations, the general public, and public interest groups. Once you determine who belongs in that group of stakeholders, your next task is to ascertain whether each has a high or low interest in the project; that is, do the stakeholders support the project or are they against it? Another key consideration is their level of involvement, and when that involvement might occur: Is the stakeholders' involvement high or low? Definite or maybe? Finally, determine their ability to influence project success: Is it high or low? How much power do the stakeholders have?

Stakeholders should also be viewed for what they can bring to the table. For example:

➡ Resources, people, equipment, or supplies needed to execute the project

➡ Information to help define the result of the project

➡ Expertise to do the project work

The project manager will spend a lot of time interacting with stakeholders and managing their expectations.

PLANNING A PROJECT

At first, a project can seem amorphous if it comes from a stakeholder like a customer who has only a general notion of what the project should accomplish. For example, "We want you to upgrade our computer system" does not qualify as a good project description. Most customers do not have a precise idea of what they want, but in most cases, they sure know what they *don't* want. This is the root of one of a project's greatest challenges.

Your first job, therefore, is to set about translating the stakeholder's needs into requirements, which in turn define the project. This is the *scope* of the project. Without this step, the project is bound for failure.

There are three closely related definitions for scope. It's extremely important that all parties have a clear understanding of the term and how it's being used. The following definitions come from the *PMBOK Guide:*

1. **Scope** is "the sum of the products, services, and results to be provided as a project."

2. **Product scope** refers to "the features and functions to be included in a product, service, or result."

3. **Project scope** is "the work that must be done in order to deliver

a product, service, or result, with the specified features and functions."

Ultimately, the amount of time spent defining the scope of the project should be proportional to the project's importance to the organization and the project's size, complexity, and risk. Balance time and merits when defining the scope of a project.

This exercise produces a *scope statement*. The goal of the scope statement is to ensure that requirements are quantified and properly linked to the project's goals and objectives and that the project is completely defined. This can be a challenge if the stakeholder has provided only limited or unclear information about requirements. To get the job done right, you may need to put a subject matter expert on the project team in direct contact with the stakeholder. Example: For an IT project, the customer requires a user-friendly graphical user interface (GUI). The requirement is ambiguous, so the team member specializing in construction of GUIs works with the customer—ideally the end-user—to define what the GUI should look like and how it should function from an end-user's perspective.

The scope statement describes, in detail, the project's deliverables and what must be accomplished to create them. It becomes the basis for more detailed planning of the project. At a minimum, the project's scope statement should address the following areas:

- Deliverables of the project (the new product, service, or result)

- Description of the product (product scope)

- Acceptance criteria for the product (criteria that must be met for the customer to accept the result of the project)

- Project exclusions (things that are not within the scope of the project)

- Project constraints (things that limit the team's flexibility)

→ Project assumptions (things assumed to be true for planning purposes that must be confirmed/validated at a later time)

Together, the project charter and scope statement provide information describing:

→ Intended result(s) of the project

→ Business or technical rationale for undertaking the project

→ Project's alignment with strategic business issues

The concept of *requirement is central in these critical project documents.* The *PMBOK* definition is this: A requirement is "a condition or capability that must be met or possessed by a system, product, result, or component to satisfy a contract, standard, specification, or other formally imposed document." In other words, requirements formally define project completion and success criteria and define the functional characteristics of the products and services.

In Chapter 2 on Performance Management, in the discussion of "the process of managing," the acronym SMART was used to describe a set of good performance objectives. Similarly, the acronym applies to project management. The slight variation on the meaning of the letters as they pertain to project requirements is as follows:

Specific

Measurable

Agreed-to

Realistic

Time-bound

With your project charter and scope statement in hand—and a clear understanding of project requirements—you are ready to move through the next steps of project planning: work breakdown, estimates on time and money needed for each piece of work, the project schedule, roles and responsibilities of all participants, and risk analysis.

A *work breakdown structure* (WBS) is an outline of the work needed to meet project objectives; that is, all of the work that needs to be done on the project, including project work and product work. Large, complex projects are organized by breaking them down into progressively smaller pieces until they are a collection of defined work packages (WPs) that may include a number of activities. Keep in mind that:

➤ Creating the WBS is simple but not always easy.

➤ The outline is logical and hierarchical but not necessarily sequential.

➤ At its highest level, the WBS conveys an approach, strategy, methodology, template, or best practice routinely used in your type of project.

➤ At its lowest level of detail, the WBS has unique work packages that must be performed.

Because the project manager (PM) is accountable for most project-related documentation and deliverables, the PM is ultimately responsible for the creation of the WBS as well as the activities list that goes with it. But the PM doesn't do all of the work. The project manager leads the effort to create the WBS, but it is often left up to team members—sometimes with the help of others in their functional areas—to create the part they will be responsible for. The subject matter experts on the team are often more knowledgeable about the work that needs to be done.

The outline of a WBS is an organization chart of the work, similar in structure to the organization chart for people that illustrates relationships and hierarchy. The following example is for a project that takes the form of a symposium:

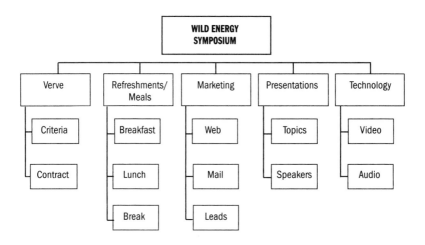

Every box on the chart is "owned" by someone, some team, or some department. As noted previously, the WBS chart does not address sequence; there may be lateral handoffs of work products from one area to another, and the chart does not necessarily capture this kind of collaboration. The WBS outline, therefore, is not a stand-alone document. A full project WBS lists the following for each of the five project phases (concept, plan, development, execution, and closing):

→ Deliverables

→ Work packages

→ Activities

The activities list accompanying the WBS provides necessary detail on actions required to carry out the project. While the development of the WBS and the activities list are two separate components of project planning, they are most often done concurrently.

In terms laid out in the *PMBOK*, a full project WBS would convey the relationship of deliverables to work packages to activities as the following outline suggests:

Phase 1

    Deliverable 1.1
        WP 1.1.1
            Activity 1.1.1.1
            Activity 1.1.1.2
        WP 1.1.2
    Deliverable 1.2
        WP 1.2.1
        WP 1.2.2
            Activity 1.2.2.1
            Activity 1.2.2.2

You would repeat the layout for each phase.

In the example just given, Deliverable 1.1 might be selecting the venue, which would be supported by determining eligible sites, with the activities being site visits and negotiations with property managers. The roles of different people having to do with the "ownership" of the boxes would necessarily involve one or more of the stakeholders in determining basic criteria for the venue, and the involvement of at least one other person, perhaps a meeting planner. So, if the stakeholders decided the conference should occur roughly in the middle of the country and be able to accommodate 100 people, then the meeting planner might begin with a long-distance evaluation of facilities in Denver, Colorado. The next activities would be visiting a select number of properties, eliminating those that don't meet the group's needs, and getting bids from the rest.

Concurrently, a colleague such as the manager of education programs might begin lining up speakers based on knowledge of the purpose of the conference, the city in which it will be held, and the conference dates.

Keep these guidelines in mind when developing the WBS:

→ The level(s) of detail of the WBS should be dictated by the size, complexity, and risk of the project.

→ The level at which you plan establishes the level at which, thereafter, you can control the project.

→ One person's project may be another's work package.

→ Too much detail can be counterproductive.

Regarding this last point, large or complex projects may require quite a bit of detail and your team may want to create a *WBS dictionary*. This document contains more detailed information concerning the various elements in the WBS and is viewed as a useful resource by project managers, team members, and other stakeholders. At a high level, the dictionary may only include a brief description of the WBS elements. If the WBS is extensive, the dictionary may include other information, such as:

→ Associated activities

→ Milestones to gauge progress

→ Responsible organization

→ Scheduled start and end dates

→ Required resources (equipment, supplies, materials, people, specialties)

→ Estimates

→ Quality information (acceptance criteria, performance measurements)

Review what you have accomplished in the planning phase to this point: the project charter, scope statement, and work breakdown. To complete the planning phase, you now need estimates on time and money needed for each piece of work, the project schedule, roles and responsibilities of all participants, and a risk analysis.

The key to successful estimating is being as accurate as possible—not padding estimates. Here are five guidelines for achieving accurate estimates:

1. *Understand exactly what is expected of you for each activity.* Compose a complete description of the product(s) you are creating, down to the last detail. Specify exactly when it is due. Communicate who needs to know what and when they need to know it. Have a clear idea of the administrative requirements related to the project; that is, what documentation is required. Finally, determine the quality-control requirements: Against what standards should you measure the product, and which of these standards must be met before the project is considered complete?

2. *Understand the difference between effort estimates and duration estimates.*

- **Effort estimates** refer to the amount of actual labor required to perform the task. That labor might be associated with a single individual or with more than one, but the estimate captures the time it would take to do the activity regardless of how many people participate.

- **Duration estimates** are how much time the task is expected to take on a calendar, from the time the task is started until it is completed. Know how much time you can legitimately dedicate to the project activity—your "utilization" calculated as follows:

$$\text{Utilization} = \frac{\text{Time of Actual Work}}{\text{Total Duration}}$$

So, if the activities that take you away from the project require 30 percent of your time, you can run, at best, at a 70 percent utilization rate. Your productivity is 70 percent. A task that would take you 10 days without interruptions would really take you 14 to 15 days—to be exact, 14.286 days (which is 10 divided by 0.7).

3. *Understand administrative, communication, and quality-control requirements for the activity.* As part of a project team, other team members rely not only on the quality of your work, but also on the information you provide them.

4. *Adjust for experience, complexity, risk, visibility, and number of people.* Regarding this factor, here are some commonsense reminders:

- The more complex the activity is, the more work it will require.

- The more visible the activity is, the more communication and interruptions you will have to handle.

- The riskier the activity, the greater the probability for delays and additional work.

- The level of experience of the person performing the work is what counts, not your own experience level. (Remember, you may be estimating for others.)

- The more you do something, the quicker you become at doing it. (In other words, factor in learning curves.)

- The more people on the activity, the more effort it will take. (You will need to communicate, coordinate, and resolve conflicts that wouldn't exist if done by only one person.)

5. *When in doubt, break it down into smaller elements.* Usually, the smaller the unit of work, the more accurate the estimate.

Next on the project planning agenda is building the project schedule. The project manager and team can proceed to building the project schedule as soon as:

➔ The WBS has been created.

➔ The activities to produce the deliverables in the WBS have been identified.

➔ Duration estimates for each of the activities have been made.

One of the first considerations is to determine the dependencies among the activities. The ability to start on one work package often depends on another being completed. There are three types of dependencies to consider:

1. **Mandatory Dependencies.** You can't put up the walls until the house is framed, and you can't frame the house until the foundation is laid. This is called *hard logic.*

2. **Discretionary Dependencies.** You may want to reflect best practices or take an alternative approach because of some unique circumstances. This is called *preferred logic* or *soft logic.*

3. **External Dependencies.** You're dependent upon something external to the project. Work Package 1.1 is completed on the seventeenth of the month, and Work Package 2.1 could start on the eighteenth, but the parts won't arrive from overseas until the twenty-second.

The Critical Path Method (CPM) is the most common technique for building a project schedule and it is supported by most project management software. It's a way of setting priorities and scheduling a set of project activities and can be used for any project that has interdependencies. CPM shows not only the amount of time a task will take, but also the amount of time a task can be delayed or "float" on a calendar without affecting the project completion date.

Float is the amount of time that a deliverable can be delayed without causing a delay to other work packages *(free float)* or the project completion date *(total float).* Tasks with float time are less critical to the schedule than those without float, which is why CPM is an excellent tool for setting priorities.

The *critical path* is the path made up of activities that have zero float. These activities must start on time and finish on time for the project to be completed on time. They have no flexibility. The critical path also determines the soonest a project can be completed, so it's the longest path in the project.

While most of the focus may be on tasks along the critical path, that doesn't mean tasks on the other paths in the project can be ignored. If tasks are delayed more than their float, the critical path changes.

This logic diagram may help clarify the principles in action:

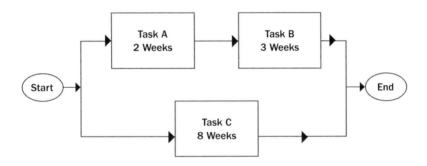

If Task C will take eight weeks, and Tasks A and B will only take five weeks combined, they have a float of three weeks. It is therefore critical to make Task C a priority and ensure it starts and ends on time, because a delay on Task C jeopardizes the entire project schedule.

Experienced project managers have also developed an "official" way of displaying the project schedule; it's called a Gantt chart. It's critical that you understand how to read a Gantt chart when you see it so that you can see the dependencies as well as track your own work against the plan. You may also be required to maintain a presentation of the schedule for your portion of the project.

Using a Gantt Chart

→ Each activity is represented by a bar. The length of the bar represents its duration.

→ Activities bars are connected using lines and arrows.

→ The start of the project is on the left and the end is on the right.

→ Activities on the critical path are normally in red.

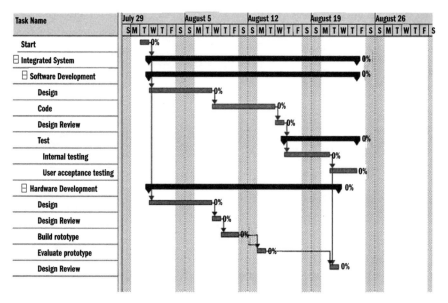

Source: Microsoft product screenshot, reprinted with permission from Microsoft Corporation.

For those team members, sponsors, and senior levels that don't respond well to Gantt charts, such as the one shown here, a calendar approach is an alternative. The calendar view gives team members/ readers the time frames for their tasks along with the duration, for a better frame of reference. The data is the same; however, the view has changed to something more traditional—that is, a simple calendar with notes on it about when certain activities start and end, and when certain deliverables are due.

There are project management software packages available to help project teams produce usable project schedules. Some are easy to use, while others are very complex. Some have limited functionality, and others are robust, providing multiple ways besides a Gantt chart and calendar to display a schedule. Regardless of the software package you use, remember it is a tool. You manage it—don't let it manage you.

Having identified what needs to be done during the project, the next consideration is roles and responsibilities. Ask the questions: Who is going to do it? Who has to answer for the result? Whom do we need to consult with or keep informed?

A common tool used to connect people with the work on the project is a Responsibility Assignment Matrix (RAM). Key terms (and their definitions) used in relation to RAM include:

→ **Role.** The portion of a project a person is accountable for; the part the person plans (e.g., a project manager may function as business analyst, or a functional manager may be assigned as a subject matter expert).

→ **Responsibility.** Work that a team member is expected to do; who does the work.

→ **Accountability.** Who is answerable for the results.

→ **Competency.** The skill and capacity needed to do the work.

→ **Authority.** The right to do something (e.g., make decisions, spend money, approve requests).

The final component of the planning phase involves an assessment of risk associated with the project. A risk is an uncertain event or condition that, if it occurs, has a positive or negative effect on a project's objectives. Risk is not necessarily bad; it just needs to be analyzed in the context of the project and there needs to be a plan to handle it—to mitigate the negative impact or boost the positive effect.

Risks are present on all projects. There is a probability they will occur and an impact if they do. As part of project planning, the project manager creates a risk management plan that details how risk activities will be carried out over the course of the project. In addition to identifying risk activities and determining when they should occur, the project manager, along with the project management team and other people with risk responsibilities, will review the templates and tools used to identify, analyze, document, and plan for risks.

Once risks are identified, they are documented on a *risk register.* Initially, very limited information about the risks may be available; however, it might be obvious what would cause the risk and how to respond to it, so it's appropriate to document those conditions immediately. The risk register is then used to capture additional information during the other risk activities.

Here is an example of what the risk-register table might contain, with a heading that includes the project name and other umbrella identification information, such as a project number:

WB#	Description of Risk	Risk Category	Priority	Causes	Probability	Impact	Risk Response	Owner	Date Identified	Date Closed	Comments

RISK REGISTER TABLE

Risk analysis is a whole discipline unto itself, but the basic process of identifying project risks is uncomplicated: Brainstorm with the project team. Each subject matter expert on the team should have a clear sense of the qualitative risks associated with the SME's area of expertise.

Once risks have been analyzed, response plans have to be developed. The responses should be appropriate and based on priority, cost, and timing.

There might be some risks of such high severity that you want to totally avoid or prevent them. In this case, the approach might be to change the plan or change the schedule.

For a lesser-priority risk, you might consider some form of mitigation strategy to reduce the probability or impact of the risk. For example, if there is risk that one of the vendors might have difficulty meeting its delivery schedule for parts, the planned response might be to identify an alternative vendor. Additionally, there will probably be some risks that are rated low priority, based on their probability and impact scores. These risks might not warrant any response plan and would be dealt with when and if they occur.

As a final note, be sure to differentiate between risks and issues. An issue is a point or matter that is in question, in dispute, or under discussion because there are opposing views or disagreements. Document and discuss issues to ensure that they do not become negative project risks, or else to turn them into risks with a potential for positive effect.

EXECUTING A PROJECT

Once the project plans have been reviewed and approved, the project team members, under the direction of the project manager, go about working the plan and accomplishing the tasks and work assignments delegated to them.

Let's review elements of the project and the actions that need to occur in relation to them:

→ Work must be authorized and performed according to the approved plan.

→ Information must be collected to determine the current status of the project.

→ Variances between the plan and actual status must be identified and analyzed.

→ Causes for variances must be identified.

→ Corrective actions, if any, must be developed and assessed.

- Recommended corrective actions must be reviewed, approved, and implemented.
- Project plans must be updated and communicated.

To be successful, project managers must be armed with current and accurate information. In that role, you should have several tools at your disposal to acquire current information regarding the status of your project:

- Status reports
- Status meetings
- MBWA (management by walking around)

The project's communication plan often prescribes the types of reports and meetings the project manager will use, including their format, frequency, level of detail, and source. In designing a status report, create a format that guides team members in delivering pertinent information, and be sure to specify how often the report needs to be updated. Some of the topics or sections for inclusion in these reports might be:

- Completed tasks
- Tasks started and not yet completed
- Tasks started late
- Tasks not completed and that are beyond their scheduled completion dates
- Deliverables completed
- Overdue deliverables
- Key accomplishments during the current reporting period
- Key accomplishments for the next reporting period

→ Action items assigned

→ Issues assigned

→ Risks assigned

→ New risks identified

→ Additional resources needed

→ Changes implemented

→ Changes requested

When addressing these topics, you may have to provide dates, such as:

→ Scheduled start date

→ Scheduled completion date

→ Actual start date

→ Actual completion date

It's common practice to use color codes in status reports:

COLOR	STATUS
Green	Everything is on track.
Yellow or Amber	Things are a little behind but should get back on schedule.
Red	Real problems. Dates have been or will be missed.

Project managers may also create and/or provide other, very specific status reports for key project stakeholders. Risks, issues, and changes are common topics for these other reports.

As part of planning for communications during the project, the project manager often creates a matrix outlining the communications flow for the project. It identifies the many stakeholders on the project, who normally communicates with whom, and how often the communication normally takes place. Using this communication responsibility tool, not only can you see how information flows in the project, but the hierarchy of the titles or roles for the project as well, which is why a matrix (such as the one shown here) is often used in conjunction with a communications plan to track the project's communications.

		REPORT TO					
		Client	Acct. Mgr.	Sponsor	PM	Team	VP
Initiator	Client		●	■		□	□
	Acct. Mgr.	●		□		■	□
	Sponsor	■	□		●		○
	PM	●	●	●		●	○
	Team	□	□	□	●		■
	VP	■		■		■	

Legend:

● Weekly

● Semi-Monthly

○ Monthly

□ As needed

■ Never

The logical complements to good reports are good meetings. Every project manager needs to hear how the project is progressing. In part, this information takes the form of the regularly scheduled status meeting. Commonly, the status meeting occurs once a week, but the scope and duration of the project may alter that schedule.

In addition, when you get to a stage of the project where more frequent team contact might be needed to overcome obstacles or reduce risks, then short, tightly focused status meetings could have benefit. Sometimes they take the form of stand-up meetings, which get their name from the fact that everyone stands during the meeting. If some members of the project team work remotely, then people in the office may stand around a computer with a video link to their off-site teammates. These quick status meetings give everyone a chance to answer three questions:

1. What did I accomplish yesterday?

2. What will I accomplish today?

3. Is there anything that will prevent me from accomplishing what I plan to do today?

As a formal mechanism of project control, the status meeting is necessary, and there are two rules to adhere to: 1) The project manager listens, and 2) the project team members report the status of their work.

Refer to Chapter 1 and the guidelines on "running effective meetings" in the section on Purposeful Communication. These guidelines will serve you well for status meetings related to a project. Note, too, that it's always important to allow time for Q & A.

In addition to status meetings, you also want to have phase and gate review meetings.

Projects are broken into phases to make them more manageable. One of the elements that contributes to this increased manageability is the phase review meeting, which is held at the end of each phase of the project. This type of meeting is usually attended by the project manager, the project management team, and other key stakeholders. Certain team members, depending upon their role on the project, may also have the opportunity to attend. The agenda for the phase review, including the areas to be presented and discussed, should have been determined during the planning for the project. The umbrella items on the agenda are project performance to date and project future performance.

One difference between a phase review meeting and a gate review meeting might be the use of a Gate Review Board (GRB). Instead of presenting project performance to the key stakeholders, as in a phase review meeting, the project manager presents information to a pre-defined GRB that is often made up of vice-president or director-level personnel from across the organization. Based on the GRB's review of the project deliverables and other project information such as budget performance or quality measurements, the board votes on whether the project should pass through the gate. Each member of the board gets one vote.

Additionally, in some applications of this approach, certain other well-documented and agreed-to criteria must be met. While the criteria are organization- and project-specific, they could include positive results from a feasibility study or completion of a detailed market analysis. If the criteria aren't met, the project doesn't move forward.

Another difference is focus. More emphasis is placed on the business aspects of the project at gate review meetings. Phase reviews are more technical.

Projects that have a larger impact on the business move forward, while lower-performing projects are put on hold or "killed." So, potential for the organization, risk, and investment in the right project are all major concerns.

Invariably, action items will surface during the course of meetings that are not significant enough to add to the project activities list, but they are nonetheless things that need to get done. Assign someone to take care of these items and commit them to an action log, along with a due date for completion. Similarly, when issues arise, assign someone to address them and put them into an issue log to keep track of them. Escalate the issue if it can't be resolved at the project level by an established date.

As a final consideration, be prepared to manage change. Chapter 3 on Managing Staff Changes addressed the challenge of helping staff members adjust to shifts in human resources requirements. That foundation discussion of leading people through organizational change applies to change management within a project as well. To that guidance, add the concept of change control. Also consider that project change often originates from within the project team, rather than being something that is imposed on the team.

Project team members are often the source of undocumented and unapproved change. In their effort to provide the customer with the best product possible, they might add features and functionality without going through the formal change control process. This is called *scope creep*, and it can start as early as with the creation, review, and approval of the first project documents.

Change control is:

→ Identifying the change

→ Documenting the change

→ Approving or rejecting the change

→ Controlling changes to the project plan

A formalized process, which should be put in place at the beginning of the project, ensures that all change management recommendations— and decisions—are documented from the start.

A simple change control process may include the following steps:

1. Determine the current version of the execution plan.

2. Receive the change request.

3. Enter and update a change control log or journal.

4. Determine whether to process the request.

5. Assess the impact of the proposed change on plan parameters, such as:

   • Schedule

   • Costs

   • Asset usage

- Resource usage

- Exposure (or risk)

- Effect on other (project or nonproject) work

6. Prepare recommendations.

7. Submit recommendations for review and approval.

8. Obtain approvals.

9. Update project plans.

10. Distribute updated plans (i.e., communicate the change).

11. Monitor and track against the new plan (i.e., establish a base-line).

Once the change control process has been set, the project manager should communicate the change control requirements to all project stakeholders. From that point on, you should operate on the basis that only approved change requests will be implemented.

COMPLETING A PROJECT

After all of the work has been done to create the project deliverables and the deliverables have been turned over to the customer, it's time to close the project.

Project managers often have tools such as procedures, guidelines, and checklists to guide them through the process of closing the project. An important point to remember is that there is still more work to be done to bring the project to an end and the project manager can't do it alone. While some team members may be released back to their organizations, others will remain with the project to help with the close.

Among the administrative activities associated with closing out a project are:

→ Capturing lessons learned. These are the good things to repeat, bad things to avoid, and recommendations for future efforts.

→ Gathering and archiving project records. Warehouse plans, reports, calendars, and logs are needed to create some form of knowledge database for use on future projects.

→ Reporting on staff performance. Project managers often provide feedback to functional managers on the performance of the team members, either during the project (for projects that have a long duration) or at the end of a project.

→ Releasing the staff.

→ Closing out the financials.

A checklist to address individual items, such as "All known problems, errors, and omissions have been fixed" and "All technical documentation is complete," is also useful when it's time to close out a project.

Regardless of the reasons, canceled or terminated projects still need to go through closure. While some actions will be abbreviated and others omitted, the closure procedure and checklist (shown here) should be followed and accomplished.

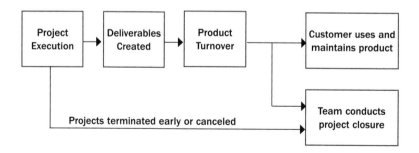

Don't forget an important thing as you close out a project. As a manager—and remember that means coach, leader, and many other roles—you need to remind people of the meaning of their work and their value to the effort. Acknowledge people individually, as well as credit the team with success or at least important lessons learned.

The following are two case studies, one of a project having a healthy amount of complexity and very few people to carry out the activities, and the other a project with an extraordinary amount of risk and very few people to carry out the activities. In both cases, the project teams succeeded because of the ability of people to grasp firmly the problem/opportunity at hand, the interrelatedness of work packages, and the interplay of constraints, among other fundamentals of project management.

Case Study 1: Moderate Complexity Project

In its infancy, WatchGuard Technologies was a start-up business of about two dozen people with one project: Gain market acceptance for a revolutionary network security device. The very fact that it was a plug-in device, not software with limitations related to the operating system, made it unique. But as customers have proved time and again, "unique" is not always good in the world of technology.

The technical team followed a sequence of actions related to field-testing the product and making adjustments based on feedback. In other words, the team knew how to create a well-defined product scope (i.e., the features and functions to be included in a product, service, or result).

But to "gain market acceptance," the network device most likely needed to be more than technically sound. The vice president of marketing had a sequence of work packages that included submission of the product to reviewers for testing, development of collateral materials, and a trade-show debut. But he felt something was missing in the project scope (i.e., the work that must be done in order to deliver a product, service, or result, with the specified features and functions).

The problem was this: The marketing VP could write about the product, show pictures of it, get reviewers to test it, and debut it at trade shows. But what was "it"? The device had no name other than "network security device."

And so the vice president of marketing created a new work package to add to the work breakdown structure—"Define what 'it' is"—and he shared ownership of that activity with anyone interested in contributing. The device became known as the "Firebox" and the vice president's logical next decision was to paint it red.

An integral part of the victory of the project was that the appearance alone drew curious reviewers and customers to test the technical proficiency of the product. That was the beginning of a huge success story that resulted, in large part, from excellent project planning and execution that included revisiting the WBS to make sure the appropriate sequence of actions had been outlined.

Case Study 2: High-Risk Project

A classic case of project management in which high risk prevailed was the successful coordination of NASA engineers' work on the ground with that of the three astronauts on the troubled Apollo 13 mission to the moon.

Michael Dobson, a noted project management trainer and author, tells the dramatic story of the Apollo 13 rescue effort from the unique perspective of a Project Management Professional (PMP). It's a situation many people can relate to, not necessarily because they've read books and articles about this space mission, but because they've seen director Ron Howard's true-to-life 1995 movie of the same name that stars Tom Hanks as mission commander Jim Lovell and Ed Harris as Gene Kranz, the NASA flight director who becomes the project manager of the rescue mission.

The pivotal scene, from a project manager's point of view, is when the engineers are gathered in a conference room. Gene Kranz enters with an assistant carrying a huge box. They dump the box full of odds and ends on a table. Kranz announces they have a problem; they have to shut down the command module and move the astronauts into the

Lunar Excursion Module (LEM). Unfortunately, the LEM was only rated to keep two people alive for a day and a half, so the problem/opportunity was to figure out how to keep three astronauts alive for four days in the LEM. Without any spare carbon dioxide scrubber filters for the LEM, that didn't seem possible. The astronauts had lots of filters for the command module, but they were square and the ones needed for the LEM were cylindrical.

The project title might therefore be Putting a Square Peg in a Round Hole. And this engineering feat had to be accomplished before the CO_2 rate reached a toxic level of 15, a reality that would happen very quickly. Kranz warned the NASA engineers gathered, "Failure is not an option." It's easy to imagine that everyone in the room thought, "Failure is option number one."

Focus immediately goes to the biggest issue in project management, the triple constraints. It is the iron triangle of time, cost, and scope requirements.

Those gathered needed to know exactly why time was a major and inflexible constraint. When the CO_2 level reached 15, all three astronauts on board would become impaired. When that happened, they would not be able to build whatever the engineers on Earth designed to mitigate the problem. Of course, the ill effect could occur at a level of 14.8 or 15.5; in short, the time constraint was not guided by a precise measurement.

And in this case, it was unfair to say that cost was not an issue. Spending all the money in the world wouldn't have solved the problem, but resources were definitely needed. The cost constraint came down to what was in the box that Kranz and his assistant had dumped on the table. That collection of odds and ends represented what the astronauts *probably* had to work with to effect their makeshift repairs and return to Earth safely. In effect, that collection of items was the project budget. But the project manager could not have a firm grasp on this constraint either, because there was no certainty that the items in the box matched those on the ship exactly.

As for the next major constraint, the scope requirement was clear:

This project involved activities to save the lives of the astronauts. Nothing else was relevant.

Now consider the additional three key constraints as listed earlier in this chapter: risk, resources, and quality. Resources were already addressed as part of the cost discussion.

Next, look at quality. This project provides a perfect example to see how quality need not only be defined by performance. In some cases, such as that of Apollo 13, an element inherent in quality is speed. If the engineers found an elegant solution to the problem that took a day to build, it would be analogous to going to the emergency room with heart failure and being told, "We have a great cardiologist who works with us here in the emergency department. He's on duty next Tuesday." Another key characteristic of quality in this case was value; that is, the desired return on investment. With the Apollo 13 situation, having speed and value meant that the astronauts would live. Without them, they would die.

It was not a matter of how good the solution would be, but what the "good enough" point was. A key part of "good enough" in the Apollo project centered on the fact that the astronauts wore socks that could be repurposed as air filters. One of the big lessons here is for a project team to have a comprehensive inventory of everything that could be useful in making a project succeed.

"Good enough gives a lot of project managers trouble because they go into denial," says Dobson. "They protest: 'Good enough isn't.' That gives me a problem because if 'good enough isn't,' then it seems to me that good enough has not been properly defined."

In a finite, constrained project environment, such as that faced by the Apollo combined team of astronauts and engineers on the ground, establishing a precise description of "good enough" is crucial. In short, you should know what defines "good enough" even if you plan to exceed it.

We know the teams in space and on the ground succeeded, but describing how they did it from a project management perspective is a different twist. Central to their victory was exploiting the final constraint risk.

Awareness of the most significant risk—that is, the death of the astronauts—spurred the project team to ask "what if?" questions. The result quickly yielded multiple scenarios guiding their swift response, which embodied both logic and imagination.

That is a key lesson on project management to take from this story. A successful project is often not the product of formulas; rather, it's the product of human talent, skill, and experience using the benefit of structure to put it all together.

SECTION I ACTION ITEMS

Whether you currently have managerial responsibilities or anticipate a promotion in the near term, allow yourself time and space to implement the guidance in the preceding chapters incrementally.

❏ *Start with a self-assessment.* Reflect on the eight roles of managers and what you may be predisposed to handle well, as opposed to those types of responsibilities you will need to cultivate. Rather than try to "show off" what you're good at, aim for balance. All eight roles need your 100 percent effort.

❏ *Identify the three or four actions that, when taken, will quickly increase your effectiveness and that of your direct reports.* Improving written and oral communication, including the ways meetings are conducted, are areas where you should experience immediate results.

❏ *Set priorities on implementing the recommendations in the chapters.* Once you recognize that a serious problem exists in the environment or with employee motivation, for example, you can focus on actions to create a healthy environment and help employees rise to their highest level of competence and commitment.

❏ *Work as a member of a team.* Functioning in isolation will not yield the personal and professional growth that working with a mentor and/or respected colleague will provide. In trying to develop the essential management skills presented in this section, look to role models to demonstrate ways to learn and apply these skills in your organization.

Cont'd.

SECTION I ACTION ITEMS

❑ *Examine closely what goes into making a project successful.* Use your new perspective as a project manager to see what makes a conference or product launch work or fall short. When you watch documentaries, movies, or television shows, consider what element of the story involves a project and pay attention to how well or poorly those responsible handled it. Keep a mental inventory, or perhaps even a physical list, of what you've observed as keys to success or reasons for failure.

SENIOR MANAGEMENT SKILLS

You do not have to be in a senior management position to need senior management skills. In balancing your roles between operational management and strategic thinking, you sometimes need to adopt the mindset of a visionary, even though you may not formally serve a strategic planning role in your organization. You also need to infuse your operational management with leadership skills. Remember the eight roles described in Chapter 1? You enrich your ability to step into those roles and give a "command performance" by cultivating the senior management skills covered in this section.

CHAPTER 5

Strategic Thinking

The expectation in most organizations is that all team members will be and should be involved in thinking strategically about the roles they currently play in the firm and the roles they could or should play in the future. This expectation applies to every manager, whether you have direct reports, manage a process, or act as a project manager on a cross-functional team. The intent is not for you to take the guidance in this chapter and become a strategic planner for your company. Rather, the focus is on helping you develop a strategic mindset for your particular work unit.

WHY MANAGERS NEED TO THINK STRATEGICALLY

The shift toward a strategic mindset is essential for managers who must help their organizations succeed in an environment of continual change. While ultimately driven by the marketplace, companies must also respond to changes in the economy, technology, social and lifestyle choices, the political landscape, and global competition. As a result, the very nature of organizations is changing. Organizational structures have been turned upside down, flipped, stretched, and compressed.

The way information and ideas flow needs to change to reflect this dynamic nature of today's organizational structures. Senior management is listening as well as telling; it is watching as well as showing; and it is expecting employees at all levels to be producers (and not just users) of information, new ideas, and solutions.

Employees at all levels should be encouraged to develop, suggest, and implement new strategies for:

→ Increasing organizational effectiveness

→ Reducing costs

→ Improving customer service levels

→ Making a positive contribution to the bottom line

As organizations continue to flatten, the traditional role of the manager has undergone a dramatic redefinition. Previously expected to simply execute tasks, plans, decisions, and policies made by senior management, operational managers are now asked to participate in the planning process as well. That means they must understand the direction of the organization, foreseeing potential problems and challenges that are on the horizon while also offering solutions and strategies for dealing with an uncertain future.

Strategic contributions take shape in such areas as creating a vision for the organization, effectively utilizing and capitalizing on resources to implement activities needed to move toward the vision, fostering innovation through conversations that reflect diverse points of view, and continually asking "what if" to keep employees sensitive to the ever-changing needs of customers and tactics of competitors.

Here's a real-world example: A group of software engineers representing technology companies of all sizes was considering adopting the work of a member company and submitting it to the American National Standards Institute (ANSI) so that it could become a national standard. They would simply have to vote to accept the technical specification that addressed how to make computers more secure and forward their voting results to ANSI. When news of the specification went public, a backlash ensued; some people thought the action had less to do with security and more to do with prohibiting people from legitimately sharing information stored on their computers. Many people on the standards committee wanted to get on with the process quickly and get it over with. The chairman of the committee, however, decided to issue a press release to make sure that the very people who criticized the move could not only attend the meetings, but also vote if they joined the committee. Some of the committee members thought he had lost his mind, and the result surprised them. The action succeeded in bringing in new members to the group and revising the specification in question. Instead of taking a task-oriented, get-through-the-agenda approach, he kept his eyes on the true purpose of the committee, which was to involve "all interested parties" in the work of computer security, and he got the work done while raising the reputation of the committee.

A STRATEGIC FRAME OF REFERENCE

One of the key characteristics of a strategic thinker is the ability to think concurrently along dual tracks. A strategic thinker must consider and incorporate data that may include *short- and long-term challenges, systems and people*, and *innovation and imitation*. This can be challenging to an operational manager since these factors often appear to be in conflict with one another. An effective strategic thinker/manager makes decisions and takes actions, having constantly explored and considered these dualities.

To do this well, a strategic frame of reference needs to be defined and applied to the organization and its business environment. The frame of reference will guide you through the maze of options that can occur. The strategic frame of reference is a planning tool. As effective as it is in planning, though, it is also an implementation tool, to help your department or work unit and entire organization to:

➡ Establish goals.

➡ Define tasks.

➡ Clarify roles and relationships.

➡ Monitor progress.

As such, the frame of reference should be dynamic, not static. It is not simply a long-range plan, drawn up every few years by senior management and placed on a shelf. Instead, it is an evolving tool that requires periodic review.

Operational managers are familiar with operational plans, budgets, and objectives—these resources are the foundation of managerial work. Managers may also be aware of the company's long-range goals and even some of the key strategies it plans to initiate to meet its goals. They are usually stated at a high level and in a conceptual manner, lacking specific quantifiable measures or time frames.

Often these statements by the company are published, promoted, and incorporated as evidence of the culture or "spirit" of the company. Seldom, however, do these high-level statements connect directly to the actions operational managers must execute on a day-to-day basis.

The strategic frame of reference creates the framework that strategic thinkers can/should use to move their organizations into the future. It provides the working context for carrying out operational initiatives (the "what is") and creates a framework for strategically envisioning the future (the "what if").

The strategic frame of reference and its elements are illustrated in the following diagram. The form of a pyramid is used, since each level supports the one above it. The focus, though, is always on the customer or client served.

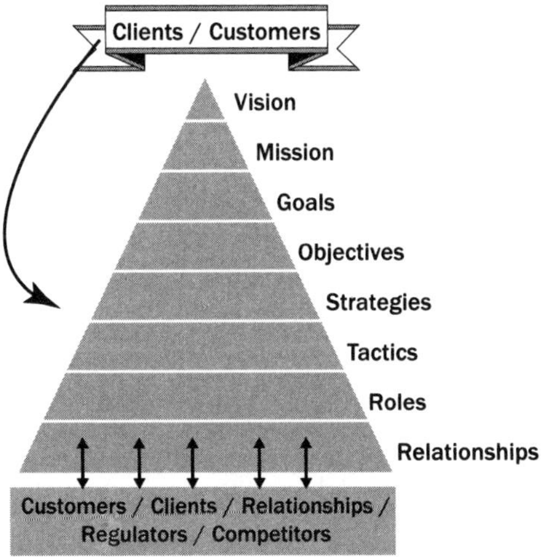

Elements of the Strategic Frame of Reference

Elements of the strategic frame of reference can be described as follows (with examples given):

- **Vision** describes where you want the company, business unit, department, or work group to be in the foreseeable future.

  Ask: *What if the work unit were to become...?* The answer should capture the values of your group and describe what is possible, with an emphasis on your group's relationship to its clients or customers. State the answer in **future** terms.

  Example:

  "We will be regarded by our clients and peers as the finest architects of traditional residential housing in the Southwest." —Large architectural firm

➤ **Mission** describes why the company, business unit, department, organization, or work group exists.

> **Ask:** *What is the purpose of our business?* The statement should cover what the company does, whom it serves, and what products and services it provides. A mission statement is stated in present terms and reflects an **existing** purpose.

> **Examples:**

>> *"Make money and have fun."* —MISSION STATEMENT OF W. L. GORE, THE GORE-TEX MANUFACTURER

>> *"ACE is a nonprofit organization committed to enriching quality of life through safe and effective exercise and physical activity."* —MISSION STATEMENT OF AMERICAN COUNCIL ON EXERCISE

➤ **Goals** are what will get you to your vision.

> **Ask:** *What if there are changes to…?* Look to the future and state overarching achievements and/or initiatives for major categories of the business that enable you to fulfill the mission. Goals are a **subjective** means of measuring progress toward the vision. They are the strategic imperatives for the company, business unit, department, or work group.

> **Example:**

>> *"Expand into the Pacific Northwest market over the next decade."*

➤ **Objectives** are the major steps you will take to achieve the goals.

> **Ask:** *How will we measure our success?* In the response, specify intended results for each goal that are specific and measurable. Any one goal may have multiple objectives that

need to be reached. Meeting specific objectives is a way of measuring progress toward the goals. These steps are **objective** means of reaching the company, business unit, department or work group's goals.

Examples:

> *"One partner will win one planning contract for a hotel or resort by the end of the next fiscal year."*

> *"One senior project manager will develop and lead an in-house staff training program for all software project staff, operational by the end of September 20xx."*

➜ **Strategies** describe how you will go about taking the steps.

Ask: *What if you...?* Articulate the options available to enable the work group to meet its objectives. Strategies are more limited in scope and more specific than goals and objectives, which are high-level and focused on long-term results. Strategies address the how-to of meeting objectives.

Examples:

> *"Develop a strategic alliance with a hotel operations consulting firm."*

> *"Instruct the senior project manager in training techniques before launching an in-house training program."*

➜ **Tactics** describe who will do what, and by when.

Ask: *What specifically will you and others do?* State your near-term and specific actions in support of the strategy.

Example:

> *"The office manager will research and recommend a seminar for training our senior project manager by July 1."*

➡ **Roles** describe the range of tasks each function must assume.

> **Ask:** *What will each function be responsible for in the operational plan?* Identify the ownership of tasks. Specify the collection of responsibilities assigned to each function in the organization—that is, the roles—so you have a clear idea of who supports the strategies and objectives of the unit and how they lend that support. Responsibilities include specific job content for people in the company, business unit, department, or work group, but in themselves should not be construed as a fixed job description.

> **Examples:**

>> *"The marketing director is responsible for researching new markets, identifying candidates for strategic alliances, defining marketing strategies by segment, and leading the production of proposals and qualification statements."*

>> *"Each principal is responsible for developing new clients, and for leading or managing a significant portion of the firm's business to meet our goals for quality and profitability."*

➡ **Relationships** describe how people work with others to be successful in achieving a common goal.

> **Ask:** *What function will be affected?* Describe the **alliances** among company members, peers, directors, consultants, customers, clients, vendors, and regulators—the working level where the strategic direction is exhibited. These relationships are the key interactions that occur among people seeking shared results. Relationships are the foundation for all efforts of the company, business unit, department, or work group. And in the end, they point back to the client as the primary focus.

Example:

> *"The project team involves everyone impacting the software development effort, both inside and outside the company, with the customer's needs and standards guiding our actions."*

No doubt, you recognized many of these terms. More important, the concepts should be familiar, regardless of what you call them. Use whatever words your organization commonly relies on. And keep in mind that there is no single "one size fits all" application of the strategic frame of reference model that can apply to all departments within an organization, or to any single department and its parent organization at the same time.

UNDERSTANDING THE OPERATIONAL MISSION

The essential elements of your operational mission are your team, your customers, and your competitors. Strategic thinking necessitates the ability to zoom out and get a big-picture view of how your team, customers, and competitors interrelate and what changes need to occur in those relationships in order to bring the vision to life and execute the mission.

Mission and vision statements are often confused. A mission describes *what you do*, but a vision describes a *desired future state*. If no change is needed or desired, then a clear mission statement will suffice. To drive change, however, you need both a clear mission and a compelling vision.

In dealing with these concepts, it is critical to realize that having a clear mission and shared vision is not limited to the company as a whole. Every business unit, department, work group, and team must clarify its existing purpose and innovate its future as part of the whole. Strategic thinkers, at all levels, seek to define these concepts for themselves and their immediate work environment.

Developing a mission statement for your group has tremendous value as you cultivate strategic thinking skills. Use the following questions and example as a guide.

Who are you?

> How is the organizational work group identified, in specific terms?

What are you?

> What is the nature of the work group?

What do you do?

> What products and/or services do you currently provide?

Whom do you serve?

> Are your customers internal, external, or both? Who are they?

Why does the organizational work unit exist?

> What value does the work group bring to its customers to support its missions?

Example:

Who you are: The refuse and recycling department of Hometown Refuse Company.

What you are: Collection refuse specialists.

What you do: Provide a refuse and recycling collection service.

Who you serve: Residential and commercial clients in Hometown, USA.

Why you exist: To ensure clean and efficient refuse removal and recycling collection.

Effective operational managers/strategic thinkers understand what's happening in their specific work group, as well as with their customers, with the competition, and in the industry. An effective tool to help you develop this view is a SWOT analysis. SWOT is the acronym for identifying your work group's specific **S**trengths, **W**eaknesses, **O**pportunities, and **T**hreats.

Strengths include skills and practices that meet your customers' most important needs and expectations. These core competencies enable you to gain superior results over time. Use them whenever possible and try to maximize them.

Weaknesses identify a shortfall in current core competencies and performance. These skills and practices must be improved in the future in order to meet customer expectations. Do what you can to minimize or eliminate them.

Opportunities surface when you understand customer needs, wants, and expectations. These opportunities will be reflected in new markets or services that can be developed to meet a need. Seize them and capitalize on them.

Threats are areas of your business where there is competitive disadvantage. These negative trends, events, or pressures must be managed in order to survive. Identify and mitigate them.

SWOT analysis has two applications: looking internally at your team and assessing your customers and competitors. This analysis can help you identify how to strengthen your partnerships or alliances with key customers. By understanding what they do well, and where they need strengthening, you can create opportunities to partner with them and provide the needed service or product support.

By understanding your team, customers, and competitors, you can create your desired future. You can make smart decisions about the utilization of your resources. Every organizational work group faces an array of opportunities and threats that will ultimately impact its future success. Your role is to find ways to maximize the opportunities and minimize/eliminate the potential threats to your future. By identifying not only the strengths and weaknesses of the work unit, but also the opportunities and threats, the operational manager/strategic thinker begins to move away from what is (mission) and begins moving toward the what if (vision).

Opportunities and threats to the organizational work group can be external or internal factors, including the following:

EXTERNAL FACTORS	**INTERNAL FACTORS**
Government	Company Structure
Environment	Culture
Politics	Politics
Society	Employee Relationships
Technology	Technology
Globalization	Outsourcing

A SWOT analysis of your competitors creates a benchmark your company can use to measure its current level of performance. This analysis also can provide direction for your team to achieve its goals in the future.

Developing an accurate SWOT analysis is all about creating a strategic advantage. But the only way that can happen is by making sure that company or organizational resources and capabilities are configured to allow the team to seize the opportunities it chooses to pursue.

THE ANATOMY OF A STRATEGIC VISION

The process of moving from "what is" to "what if" requires focus on both internal and external factors—on the future of your team and the future of your customer or client. Since all members of a company share a responsibility for providing value to their customers, strategic thinkers must develop and share a common view of the future—*a shared vision.*

By doing and repeating the SWOT analysis, you can stay tuned in to trends that will affect how you will do business in the future to respond to your customers' needs. These trends and their effects on your customers will demand changes in and adaptation from your work group or team. You will have to continually look at:

➡ What your group does

➡ How your group does its work

➡ How it can continually be improved

From scanning these trends, you can develop strategic insights that will enable you to continue providing value to your customers and clients—after all, they are the reason you have a vision and a mission. By constantly asking yourself "what if," you can design, develop, and select appropriate actions and tactics.

Understanding Customer Sensitivities

Each of your customers or client groups, whether internal or external, has a set of requirements against which your work group will be judged. Understanding those requirements is essential to identifying goals and objectives for your department, work unit, or team and developing strategies and tactics for long-term success.

While measuring customer/client sensitivities can be the subject of extensive, detailed, and time-consuming market research, you can learn

153

a great deal about your customers on an ongoing basis by looking at past and present interactions with them, paying attention to their interactions with the marketplace as well as their decision-making process, and communicating with them frequently. You also want to discuss your findings with other members of your organization (outside your own work unit) who also serve your customers, in order to observe any trends, patterns, and so on.

In developing a clear view of customer sensitivities, it is helpful to categorize customer concerns into three basic areas: needs, wants, and expectations.

1. Needs. Identify the basic requirements of the customer and what the customer needs from the products or services your department, work group or team provides. Customers and clients need your product or service to function as designed; the data you provide to be accurate; and the communication with your group to be effective. These needs are basic and often unspoken or assumed—unless you don't meet them. Don't be afraid to ask your customer, "Why did you choose us?" or some variation on that question.

2. Wants. Customer and client wants are those things that they would like to have, but don't realistically expect, at least not right now. For example, they may want lower prices, shorter delivery times, or additional product or service enhancements that you are not currently offering (or else are offering at a price they are unwilling to pay). While many customers tell you what they want, there is also a tendency to make assumptions about them. Let customers tell you what they want and resist the tendency to make assumptions about their wants.

3. Expectations. Customer or client expectations are quality and service standards that are reasonable to expect. Expectations are formed by customers' experience with your service and quality history, as well as their experience with your competitors, and by information independently gained through advertisements, media, and other sources. You can manage many of these expectations by communicating with your customers and by treating them as partners in developing your business strategies.

At this point, it's important to interject a word of caution. Although it is essential to distinguish among needs, wants, and expectations at any one point in time, it is dangerous to rely on a "single shot" analysis of your customers' sensitivities when building long-term plans and relationships. Customers' expectations are dynamic and tend to change. As you meet expectations, customers will introduce new ones.

Creating a Strategic Advantage

Operational managers are usually good at identifying the strengths of their work group. The strategic thinker is the person who can assess these strengths and balance them against the customers' desires and competitors' initiatives. It is essential that you set appropriate actions and priorities, based on the relative importance your customers attach to your products and services.

One way to do this is to develop an Importance/Performance (I/P) Matrix. With input from your customers, the I/P Matrix tells you the relative importance of their needs, wants, and expectations, and how well your work group is performing side by side with them.

The I/P Matrix is a useful tool for evaluating your competitive strengths and weaknesses through your customers' eyes. Although the more typical use for the I/P Matrix is to evaluate a company against its industry competitors, it can also be used at the work group level to examine existing levels of customer satisfaction and develop a strategic advantage.

Developing the matrix is a two-step process: You first gather data about your customers and then you map it. The questions that guide your data-gathering effort are these:

→ What are the customers' specific needs?

→ What do customers expect in the near term?

➡ What do they expect in the long term?

➡ Who else can provide the products or services that my work group now provides?

➡ How important are my products and/or services to the customers in meeting the customers' business goals?

➡ What is the relative importance of my work group's service attributes?

➡ How well are we meeting the customers' expectations?

As you gather answers to these questions, assign numerical values from 1 to 10 (1 is low; 10 is high) to each of two primary sets of considerations:

1. The *importance* to the customer of each need, want, and expectation.

2. Your own perceived level of *performance* on each item.

Construct the matrix by plotting wants and expectations on a vertical axis and performance ratings on a horizontal axis. The vertical axis becomes your "importance scale" and the horizontal, your "performance scale." The points of intersection are your key indicators of current and future success. The matrix would look something like this:

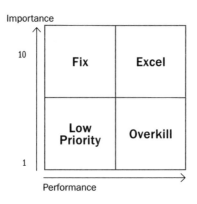

After plotting the customers' I/P dimensions, you will be able to determine which "strategic fixes" your work group will want to undertake and in what order. The plotting will be divided into four quadrants with the following definitions of potential activity:

➻ *Excel.* If your indicators fall in the upper right quadrant, you are delivering excellent performance in areas critical to your customers.

➻ *Overkill.* If indicators fall in the lower right quadrant, you may be allocating too much time to them. You should either make these needs important to the customer or spend far less effort on supporting these needs.

➻ *Low Priority.* Assign those indicators that fall in the lower left corner the lowest priority. Additional effort will do little to enhance your customers' level of satisfaction, since they place little value on results here.

➻ *Fix.* Items in the upper left quadrant, however, are things that need to be fixed. These are the true priority issues that need attention for maximum customer satisfaction and future competitive advantage.

One way to determine how to sort and assign resources to priority issues is to form a team with employees from multiple functions throughout your company and ask them to evaluate the identified issues. In deciding how to tackle these issues, go back to the SWOT analysis. A priority issue can:

➻ Exhibit a **S**trength that needs further bolstering.

➻ Uncover a **W**eakness that needs fixing.

➻ Present an **O**pportunity good enough to pursue.

➻ Highlight a **T**hreat that must be mitigated or avoided.

If you plot your scores on the I/P Matrix together with those of your competitors, you will gain valuable insight into securing a strategic advantage. When you have significantly better scores than the competition on highly important needs, you have a competitive advantage. You can continue to enhance your offerings in those areas to gain additional advantages, or at least to maintain your position. When you underperform the competition on important needs or expectations, you must make "strategic fixes" to get at least up to par. The I/P Matrix tool is helpful for this.

The I/P Matrix is helpful, but having a vision for your group is no less practical. A vision is actually a perceptible link between your current operational reality and the future. It embodies the motivation needed—and challenges involved—to get from here to there. A vision describes excellence and quality, has emotional appeal, and captures an attitude that can be shared across the internal organization and with the external customer as well.

The vision defines the desired future state of the unit. To develop this vision, determine the results, behaviors, and other characteristics the unit needs to have in the future, taking into account trends in customer needs (both external and internal customers) as well as in suppliers, vendors, and others who are involved or have a stake in the results. The vision should be continually updated as the needs of the organization and/or its customers or clients change.

A well-crafted vision helps bring focus to the people responsible for carrying out the mission and supporting the vision—but only if you, as the manager, point regularly to the linkage between current operations and the intended future. Keep the vision useful and employ it as the yardstick to measure every decision the department, work group, or team makes and the actions they take. Here are two examples of effective vision statements:

> *Loud and clear for less.*—HIGH-END COMMERCIAL AUDIO EQUIPMENT MANUFACTURER

To be regarded as advocates for the disabled, committed to enhancing the quality of people's lives through the elimination of barriers.

—NONPROFIT ORGANIZATION PROVIDING OCCUPATIONAL SERVICES

TO PEOPLE WITH DISABILITIES

The manager who thinks strategically moves the vision and mission toward implementation. To effect this outcome, involve direct reports in implementing the vision, support the group as it strives to implement the vision, and continually revisit and refine the mission to support the vision.

MAKING THE VISION A REALITY

Thinking strategically is important, but strategic thinking by itself won't result in implementation of the vision unless your skill set includes persuasive communication. The challenge that will persist throughout your service as a manager is engaging key stakeholders in actions necessary to bring the vision to life. Your role as a strategic thinker, then, is to begin the strategic conversations that will allow people to see the value they bring cross-functionally to your department, work unit, or team. As a strategic thinker, your ability to see and to discuss the connections in the system, from various viewpoints, is critical.

To a great extent, your success in persuasive communication simply involves taking advantage of the opportunities that ongoing interactions provide. By understanding these opportunities, you can engage in strategic conversations and increase their value to you and your department or team. By leveraging communication opportunities, you demonstrate a key attribute of a strategic thinker—encouraging innovation.

By listening to your customers, clients, suppliers, vendors, and workers at all levels, you can begin to build on their best ideas, thus creating greater value in the products and services you provide. Strategic thinkers stimulate innovation in others when they are open to new concepts, ideas, or approaches to their current work environment.

Your willingness to have these well-planned, strategic discussions can help accelerate the innovation process. These strategic conversations can help your department, work unit, or team gain a competitive advantage.

Three factors drive your ability to have these discussions: preparation, practice, and problem solving.

Prepare

→ Anticipate issues, questions, and concerns that others may have.

→ Collect relevant information about the company's business strategies, competitors, market trends, customers, and resources.

Practice

→ Prepare an agenda or script for the meeting.

→ Role-play the conversation with a trusted colleague.

Problem Solve

→ Focus on finding creative solutions.

→ Use probing, listening, and clarifying skills to encourage conversation.

→ Share your knowledge and expertise.

→ Encourage ownership through collaboration.

→ Reinforce participation by recognizing good ideas.

Consider the various reasons why you need to cultivate and employ persuasive abilities in trying to implement your vision. You may need others to do one or more of the following:

➤ Approve your plan.

➤ Modify it.

➤ Support it.

➤ Take part in it.

➤ Review its results.

➤ Simply learn from it.

As you craft your strategic frame of reference, once again keep these elements and their definitions in mind:

ELEMENT	**DEFINITION**
Vision	What we will be
Mission	Why we exist
Goals	What will get us there
Objectives	Major steps we will take
Strategies	How we will go about achieving our objectives
Tactics	Who will do what, by when
Roles	Ownership of tasks
Relationships	People working toward a common goal

As long as these meaningful concepts shape your strategic frame of reference—and it isn't just composed of provocative and clever words—you will have a compelling reason to be persuasive with your stakeholders.

CHAPTER 6

Leadership

As Chapter 1 noted, a key role of a manager is "leader." To handle the role well, your reliance on strategic thinking is essential since leaders adopt a big-picture view and consider day-to-day requirements in terms of mission and goals. But thinking strategically isn't enough. A leader also needs persuasive abilities to implement a vision. Leaders move their organizations forward by thinking strategically about the directions they need to take. They form relationships beyond the organization and maintain the reputation of the organization.

As you move through the material in this chapter, keep in mind that every leadership situation has three elements:

1. **A Goal**—something to be accomplished

2. **The Leader**—a person who envisions a goal to be achieved

3. **The Followers**—people who pursue the goal

Your response as a leader will depend on how these three elements work together in your organization.

LEADERSHIP SELF-ASSESSMENT

Whether you seem to be a "born leader" or are uneasy with the role of leader and need to develop leadership skills methodically, you will discover valuable insights through a self-assessment. You will want to examine your skills, traits, competencies, abilities, and experience. Since the days of the ancient Eastern and Western philosophers, such a rigorous self-assessment has been seen as the starting point for success. "Know thyself" is a key lesson of life.

The first element of a self-assessment exercise is an examination of what senior management most likely expects of you in your role as leader. Give yourself an "S" for strength or "D" for a trait that needs development. At the end of this exercise, add one or two traits that may be unique to your organization.

- [ ] Work diligently and selflessly to achieve organizational goals for performance, quality, service, profits, and civic responsibility.

- [ ] Seek out the tough jobs and take full responsibility for the outcome.

- [ ] Tackle problems head-on and find ways to overcome obstacles.

- [ ] Handle difficult employees effectively and transform them into productive members of high-performing teams.

- [ ] Align the efforts of individuals and teams with the organization's vision, values, and objectives.

- [ ] Handle crises and rapidly changing situations smoothly.

- [ ] Forecast and manage change; overcome resistance to change.

- [ ] Plan carefully and intelligently in ways that show foresight and initiative.

- [ ] Make clear, timely decisions that address critical problems directly.
- [ ] Create a climate of open communication and trust at all levels.
- [ ] Enhance the productivity and loyalty of all members of the group.
- [ ] Stimulate employees to show greater responsibility and accountability.
- [ ] Show high levels of personal energy, initiative, and integrity.
- [ ] Possess this trait unique to my organization: ___________.

Just as important in terms of your effectiveness as leader is what your direct reports expect of you. List a few traits that you believe they would want in their leader. Better yet: Ask them. Consider both the differences and similarities between what senior management expects and what your direct reports expect. For instance, direct reports are likely to have expectations that a leader should be able to:

- Create a healthy work environment in which they can perform their job.
- Manage the performance and relationships in the work unit.
- Understand their needs and desires.
- Leave them alone to do their job, but be available and supportive.
- Provide answers to their questions.
- Make decisions fairly and in consideration of their needs.
- Help solve their problems.
- Protect them from outside distracters and problems.

➔ Fight for their needs and interests.

➔ Provide them with the information, time, and resources needed to do their jobs.

Rank yourself on how well you meet these expectations as well. Where do you earn an "S"? Where do you earn a "D"?

In summary, let's compare what senior management expects from its leaders and what qualities the leader's direct reports (i.e., followers) look for.

Senior management tends to look for:

➔ **Technical Skills** (the ability to handle the technical aspects of the work)

➔ **Management Skills** (the ability to plan, organize, support, and guide work)

➔ **Interpersonal Skills** (the ability to build solid relationships and strong teams)

➔ **Desire** (the controlled ambition to be the leader of an effort to achieve goals)

➔ **Character** (the poise, judgment, and integrity to handle tough situations well)

Followers expect and respect someone with:

➔ **Competence** (the demonstrated ability to get things done)

➔ **Credibility** (the personal qualities that project trustworthiness)

When Kate McMillan assumed her position as director of standards for the Computer and Business Equipment Manufacturers Association (now called the Information Technology Industry Council), she had already worked for the two previous directors. The first had enormous respect from the stakeholders, specifically senior management and the organizations members. This former director's technical proficiency, ability to build coalitions among member representatives, and talent for managing tasks meant that those above her ranked her performance as exceptional. Her direct reports, on the other hand, felt she had one favorite in the group and penalized or demeaned everyone else. The situation became so dire under this former director that part of Kate's job was to serve as a liaison between staff members and their boss.

In selecting that director's successor, senior management went completely in the opposite direction to avoid replicating the last disaster. They hired a personable individual well liked by staff. Unfortunately, the new director's technical skills had gaps, and the stakeholders soon realized how much that impacted their effectiveness in getting their draft standards approved.

In promoting Kate to the position, senior management, members, and direct reports got the best of both worlds. Part of leadership is not just what other people think of you, however, and Kate knew that. She didn't sit in her cubicle waiting for the movers to carry her computer into the director's office. She demonstrated a key trait that senior management sought: the desire to do the job.

BEHAVIOR OF A LEADER

The behavior of leadership might best be summed up by the acronym SPARK, meaning:

Share Information.

Play to Strengths.

Ask for Input and Appreciate Different Ideas.

Recognize and Respond to Individual Needs.

Keep Your Commitments.

The need to share information is a priority in any list of leadership characteristics. In fact, one of the first notes in the *United States Army Ranger Handbook,* in the section on Principles of Leadership, addresses the obligation that leaders have to share information:

Keep your subordinates informed. Keeping your subordinates informed helps them make decisions and exercise plans within your intent, encourage initiative, improve teamwork, and enhance morale.

As a manager and a leader, you are the liaison between the organization and the team. (Note the difference in the definition of *liaison* here and in the example given previously, where Kate McMillan had to serve as liaison between team members and their boss.) If information is power, an open flow of information is shared power. It lets people know how their work helps to achieve organizational goals and why what they do matters.

Your communication needs to be inspiring as well as factual. Your team needs to understand your commitment to achieving the results, even when you might not agree with the direction or it presents a challenge or hardship for the team. No group ever made progress when the manager was not invested in the outcomes.

One of the factors consistently mentioned in surveys to assess employee engagement is "being in on things." Your team wants to know what's going on. If there are rumors, address them. If there are new business directions, share those. Show employees that they are valued by you and the organization by sharing information with them.

Here are tips to apply the *S* in SPARK to ignite commitment:

→ Be honest. Candor matters. Candor is essential to trust.

→ Treat employees like the adults they are. Adults want to know what is going on with the organization. It's about something very important to them—their livelihood.

→ Don't be afraid to reveal your own feelings. People welcome self-disclosure.

→ If times are good, share and celebrate. If times are bad, be honest and ask for ideas.

→ Don't think you have to have all the answers. If you don't know, say so. Then try to find out the facts.

→ Be open to ideas from your team. People closest to the work are the ones who know best how to accomplish it.

In playing to your strengths (the P in SPARK), you must consider not only your own strengths, but those of the people on your team. Know what your direct reports do well and then build on that. In addition, you may occasionally need to critique the performance of others to help them upgrade their performance, but it is not your job to transform them into different people.

Following are tips to apply the P in SPARK to your efforts to ignite commitment:

→ The best way to identify strengths is to connect on a human level. That doesn't mean being "best friends" with your employees; it just means showing (and sharing) an interest in people and who they are outside of work as well as on the job.

→ Friendly, casual conversation comes more easily to some managers than others. If it is not natural to you, don't fake it. Phony is even worse—and people can tell.

→ How can you develop your empathy? Try to put yourself in the other person's shoes. Think about how you would feel in a similar situation. Focus on the employee instead of yourself.

→ Looking at strengths is not "going soft." You can still hold people to high standards, make tough decisions, and be "the boss."

➔ You pay attention to other people's strengths by recognizing and acknowledging them. This is crucial for people to gain confidence and succeed.

The A in SPARK has dual meaning and serves as a reminder that you need to listen to the response to any question. Asking for input, but then also appreciating the answers, lets employees know that you care about what they think. Does every communication between you and an employee require asking first? Of course not. But when it concerns coaching, resolving issues, solving problems, or changing procedures, you will benefit greatly from gathering ideas first. The principle is simple: Treat employees like adults.

Following are tips to apply the A in SPARK to your efforts to ignite commitment:

➔ A psychological recession sets in when fear and loss of control take over. Asking people for their ideas and approaches to situations returns some of that control to them.

➔ People closest to the work have the best idea of how to do it. Let them contribute. It will make everyone's job easier.

➔ When coaching, asking questions first makes the process two-way and helps ensure the employee's commitment to improving performance.

➔ Asking questions does not mean asking rhetorical or leading questions. If you already know the answer and know what you're going to say, don't insult the employee's intelligence by asking a pointless question.

When you recognize and respond to individual needs, you must also demonstrate a third R: *respect*. Everyone is busy. There is always a new crisis or problem to solve. There is more work than there are people to do it. In the crunch of getting everything done, the easiest thing to put aside is recognition and reward. This is both dangerous and disrespectful.

In survey after survey, recognition ranks high as a factor influencing employee commitment. Recognition and rewards do not have to be huge—but they do have to be valued by the employee. And that means knowing what matters to each person on your team. In *Business Lessons from the Edge* (p. 169), author and former COO Jim McCormick advises: "The issue of what constitutes an appropriate reward or celebration plagues a lot of executives. It doesn't have to be money. It doesn't have to be a Hawaiian getaway for the family. I used to keep gift certificates for the nearby ice cream and cookie stores in my desk as a quick 'thanks for the extra effort.' People appreciated the immediate gratification of running next door and picking up freshly baked cookies."

Who is responsible for recognition and rewards that matter? You are. Employees value your time spent with them. That's a form of recognition as well. So reward and recognize regularly and for specific actions. (No one likes a generic "Great work, keep at it.")

Here are tips to apply the R part of the SPARK model to ignite commitment:

→ Make sure that recognition is genuine and tailored to what the employee values.

→ Provide rewards and recognition often.

→ Offer praise that shows you 1) are paying attention to what the employee does and 2) value the employee's work.

→ If there is a team success, have a team celebration. You can also celebrate an honest failure as a way to recognize what was learned and to send the message that innovation and risk taking are valued.

→ Understand the impact of generational differences.

Regarding this last point, most researchers agree that there are four generations currently in the workforce:

1. *The Silent Generation.* While most people born between 1925 and 1942 have left the workforce, those that remain are usually in senior, respected positions. These survivors of the Great Depression and World War II are strong believers in traditional values: family, religion, country. Sacrifice for the greater good is seen as fitting and appropriate. True to their name, the members of the silent generation are unlikely to communicate openly, preferring to keep emotions private and letting their work speak for itself.

2. *The Boomers.* People born between 1946 and 1964 were molded by the post-WWII economic expansion of the 1950s and had a hand in the cultural shifts of the 1960s. Their values include optimism, teamwork, hard work ("workaholic"), ambition, competition, success, change, support for a cause, personal growth, and questioning authority and the "system." Although many boomers have reached retirement age, great numbers remain in the workforce. They tend to be forthcoming with opinions.

3. *Generation X.* Roughly defined as people born between 1964 and 1982. They were shaped by the computer age as well as their parents' experiences of corporate downsizing and globalization. This is the generation that is coming into leadership positions. Gen Xers are generally characterized by their entrepreneurial spirit, responsibility for self, independence, creativity, diversity, techno-literacy, desire for fun, informality, self-reliance, pragmatism, and desire for work-life balance. They communicate in an open and informal manner, comfortably use e-mail and cell phones, and are given to easy socialization and information sharing.

4. *The Millennials.* The leading edge of this generation, born between

1980 and 2000, has entered the workforce. Also known as Gen Y, Nexters, or the Internet Generation, they bring with them a facility for use of the Internet, e-mail, texting, computer games, and all the other diversions made possible by technology. They want positive (and immediate) reinforcement, autonomy, positive attitudes, diversity as a way of life, easy money, civic responsibility, and self-esteem. Adept at multitasking and avid users of technology, they pursue instant and open communication and honor their comfort level with electronic/video communication. Also of importance: Millennials tend to have limited interpersonal skills and require ongoing feedback (giving and receiving).

And now to the K in SPARK: *keeping your commitments*. Nothing can break trust more quickly than failing to keep commitments. If you ask employees for ideas, the expectation is that those ideas will be acted on in some way. If you make a commitment to follow up, be sure to do so—and then get back to the employee.

Commitments are not just those responsibilities that you as a manager undertake. The organization, too, makes commitments to the employee. This "conditional commitment" is the implied promise that the organization will deliver X to the employee—salary, benefits, opportunity, and so on—for the employee's promise to deliver Y—discretionary effort, target goal, quota, time, and so on. If the organization fails to live up to its side of the bargain in some way, employees will see no reason to keep their commitments.

Here are tips to apply the K of the SPARK model to ignite commitment:

→ Follow up on employee ideas and suggestions.

→ If the conditional commitment between the organization and the employee is in jeopardy, take immediate action to reestablish the balance.

→ As the manager, you are the face of the organization. Live up to your commitments and you'll be sending the message that the organization is also living up to its commitments.

➔ You are already leading by example; make sure it's a good one.

MEASURES OF SUCCESS

Success is a by-product of character, skill, judgment, and action taken toward a specific goal. In the previous section, the behavior of a leader was captured in the acronym SPARK, but it's important to think of leadership as more than just "doing things right." Leadership is a *process involving those behaviors in the day-to-day management of your direct reports as you aim for a goal together.*

The leadership process is summed up in this diagram:

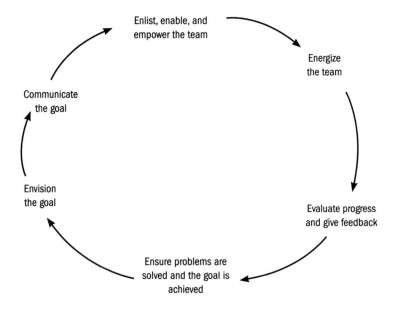

Enlist, enable, and empower the team

Energize the team

Communicate the goal

Evaluate progress and give feedback

Envision the goal

Ensure problems are solved and the goal is achieved

The success of the leader is tied directly to the success of the work and the team. It results directly from the leader generating confidence and certainty in the face of threats or challenges, getting people to take action despite their reluctance, reminding team members of the expertise they bring to the effort, and infusing them with optimism and commitment.

Here are ten critical indicators of success:

1. Accomplishment of Work

Is the work being completed to standard?

2. Increased Quality

Is the quality of work getting better?

3. Improved Teamwork

Is the team becoming stronger?

4. Improved Morale

Is the team developing a sense of pride?

5. Increased Delegation

Are you delegating more and more work?

6. Empowerment

Are you sharing power with those prepared to assume it?

7. Stabilized Systems

Are you creating systems and routines for all major processes and functions?

8. Strategic Planning and Preparation

Are you doing long-term planning and preparation?

9. Continuous Learning

Is the team learning new things?

10. Recognition and Rewards

Are people being recognized and rewarded for their contributions?

LEVERAGING YOUR LEADERSHIP STYLE

Success comes in somewhat different ways depending on the leadership style put in play. Your leadership style is defined by your interactions with others as well as the way you see yourself.

What do you focus on? Do you focus on the individuals you lead or the tasks at hand? Which is most important to you, the people or the product? Do you turn inward first when a major decision is at hand, or do you turn first to external sources of expertise or guidance?

These types of priorities—while perhaps determined only subconsciously by you—help mold your leadership style. Once you understand your leadership style, you will be better able to adapt it to the needs of others. For example, some employees may need a high degree of direction from you while others might prefer to be given a goal and then be left on their own to achieve it. In some instances, your business situation may require a certain style of leadership. In any case, you will get greater results when you adapt your style to the needs of others.

In his book *CEO Priorities*, Neil Giarratana, the former CEO of Marantec America, provides countless examples of how a leader increases his value to an organization by modifying his leadership style depending on the audience. There is no loss of consistency in behavior, but rather a genuine interest in communicating with and motivating specific people, rather than just "the employees." He emphasizes that your people are "the soul and sole power of the company," and one reason is that they have different needs and reactions. The secret is to know how to modify your leadership style to keep these different people moving in the same direction.

Variations of self-assessment instruments to evaluate your natural leadership style can be found in many books. The one described here is very simple and rooted in the Myers-Briggs Type Indicator (MBTI). In *Business Confidential*, published by AMACOM Books, former CIA case officer and certified MBTI assessor Peter Earnest cites the four Myers-Briggs personalities who are "leadership types." Each one has a somewhat different style because of the personality characteristics that are dominant. If you have taken the MBTI and know the four letters that generally characterize your personality, then you have a direct reference for assessing your leadership style. If not, you might glean very helpful insights from taking the test, which is available on a number of websites.

First, some background on the types. The basic categories are these:

→ *Introvert/Extrovert (I/E)*. The fundamental difference is how energy is directed—either inward or outward. As a corollary, extroverts feel recharged through social interaction, whereas introverts get energy from going inside their own heads.

→ *Intuitive/Sensing (N/S)*. The core issue with these distinctions is how you gather data. Your reliance on "gut feelings" (intuition) versus attention to specifications and details (as observed through the senses) establishes the distinction.

→ *Thinking/Feeling (T/F)*. This concerns how people make decisions, not whether they display no emotions or too much emotion. Thinking people have a more analytical approach than feeling people, who consider questions in terms of right or wrong, black or white.

→ *Judging/Perceiving (J/P)*. The distinction refers to how people want to manage their lives. "Judging" is not a pejorative description here. Judging personalities tend to think that there is a right way and a wrong way for situations to play out, with "right" meaning organized, structured, and uncluttered. Perceiving individuals are more open-minded in their approach and receptive to possibilities.

Plot all of the variations on a grid and the leadership types fall into the four corners. Here is the grid:

ISTJ	ISFJ	INFJ	INTJ
Do what should be done	Maintain a high sense of duty	Inspire others	See room for improvement in everything
ISTP	ISFP	INFP	INTP
Will try anything once	Hold information	Have humanitarian impulse	Enjoy solving problems
ESTP	ESFP	ENFP	ENTP
Have a high sense of realism	Live life with a sense of *carpe diem*	Want the most out of life	Embrace one challenge after another
ESTJ	ESFJ	ENFJ	ENTJ
Excel at administration	Excel at hospitality	Excel at the art of persuasion	Excel naturally at leadership

As you can see, the typical description of each type labels only one a natural leader, but the descriptions of other types (in the corner boxes) suggest different leadership styles. Consider also that people with other profiles may end up in leadership roles within an organization because of promotion, and their leadership styles may well reflect the corner they come closest to, since these sixteen types are not, in fact, cleanly defined distinctions, but rather roughly defined groupings.

Every organization has formal and information leaders, too, so one or more of your direct reports may have tremendous leadership capabilities. As a manager who has the role of leader, try to figure out how your styles complement one another and use that to your advantage in getting the team to move toward your common goal.

Let's look more closely at the four corners: ISTJ, INTJ, ESTJ, and ENTJ. Allowing for variances and exceptions depending on the environment (you may be a very different personality type at a family party and at work), which of the following best describes you?

1. I'm a private person, with a strong sense of right and wrong, who takes a careful look at the facts of the matter and has them play the lead role in shaping decisions.

2. I'm a private person, with a strong sense of right and wrong, who honors gut feelings and believes they often lead to sound decisions.

3. I'm a social person, with a strong sense of right and wrong, who takes a careful look at the facts of the matter and has them play the lead role in shaping decisions.

4. I'm a social person, with a strong sense of right and wrong, who honors gut feelings and believes they often lead to sound decisions.

This is obviously a simplistic representation of the personality types who inhabit the four corners of the grid. Nonetheless, it should get you thinking about your leadership style. And notice that the only common trait is the "judging" personality. Because perceivers are open to possibilities, it would be easy to conclude that this personality type has a place in leadership—and it does. But a leader has vision and energizes others to drive toward that vision, so the person with a sense of a right way and wrong way for situations to play out has a core leadership trait. The leader can listen and respect input about possibilities and alternatives, but that input doesn't mean changing the vision or the fundamental strategy for implementing the vision.

A leader's style should be shaped by substance, and the types of topics leaders discuss with their colleagues and direct reports suggests what that substance concerns.

➤ *Vision.* Leaders talk about their vision of the future. They paint a clear, concise, vivid, and inspiring picture of what the organization can be and what it will work toward becoming. They discuss what they want the organization to be doing extremely well in the long term.

➤ *Mission.* Leaders also talk about the organization's mission, its basic purpose, its reason for being. They describe what the organization must do day in and day out. They also show people how their work supports the attainment of the mission.

➤ *Values.* Leaders talk about their personal values and those of the organization. They describe what they stand for, what they believe in, and what they hold dear. They discuss the core principles that form the foundation for their actions. And they get followers to buy into and share these values.

➤ *Goals.* Leaders talk about SMART goals—the specific, measurable, attainable, realistic, and time-bound objectives to be achieved. They talk about goals at the organizational, departmental, team, and individual level.

➤ *Performance.* Leaders talk about current performance. They discuss what is going well and what needs to improve. They deliver reinforcing feedback to sustain good performance and corrective feedback to improve substandard performance.

➤ *Challenges and Threats.* Leaders talk about the challenges and threats the organization faces. They talk realistically about problems, obstacles, and mistakes. But they do so in a way that promotes growth and improvement.

➡ *Change.* Leaders talk about change. They discuss what must be changed, why it must be changed, how things will change, and who will be affected.

Leadership Image

Your leadership image is how people perceive your style. Acid tests of a leader's image occur when the leader is an unknown or faces a crisis. You may represent an unknown because you are walking into a new position with no previous exposure to your direct reports, or because your new management role repositions you in relation to coworkers, who must now report to you.

Just remember that you don't have to look like a superhero to be a leader. Initially, you just have to look and sound credible. That means you have to appear confident, competent, and caring. Show that you are sure of yourself, that you know what you want, and that you care about others. Over time, you must earn credibility through your actions—by *proving* you are confident, competent, and caring.

The body language of a confident leader can be summed up as follows:

➡ Stand tall or sit tall. Avoid slouching.

➡ Move with purpose; take deliberate and measured steps.

➡ Move with energy, direction, and focus.

➡ Make steady eye contact with people, but not to the extent that they think you are staring at them. It's natural and normal to move your eyes when thinking or visualizing.

➡ Smile in a relaxed and natural way. A fake smile engages only the mouth, but a genuine smile also engages the eyes.

➡ Use open gestures to illustrate your key ideas. Make sure your arms are not blocking the body. Avoid pointing your fingers or batoning with the upper arm, which is using a body part, to drive home a point. Both of these actions generally come across as aggressive or even punishing gestures.

→ Avoid invading someone's personal space. Some people may require more personal real estate than you do, depending on the culture, gender, and previous experiences of the other person. Crowding that person makes you an aggressor, not a leader.

Our speaking habits, too, are part of body language, so also keep these tips in mind as you cultivate your leadership image:

→ Speak up, project your voice, and add energy to your key points.

→ Use positive wording. Avoid negativity.

→ Don't fill the air with empty words or sounds to avoid a lull in the conversation. Silence invites comment.

→ Avoid phrases that discount or diminish the value of your ideas (e.g., *"Maybe...," "I'm not sure but...," "I could be mistaken, but..."*)

Use a style of speaking that complements your body language of confidence. Key aims are to be clear and precise, as well as credible and supportive.

→ Create vivid word pictures.

→ Get to the point.

→ Tell people the specific action steps that will lead to their success.

→ Avoid vague terms and jargon that others won't understand.

→ Show, in a nonthreatening way, that you know your subject well.

➜ Use numbers, statistics, examples, and illustrations. Cite your experiences.

➜ Use team language such as "you" and "we." Use "I" sparingly.

➜ Show an interest in the needs and desires of other people. Compliment them.

➜ Show agreement with their good ideas. Praise their efforts.

➜ Break news gently and disagree agreeably.

Your natural style of interacting may already capture a number of these points. Nevertheless, a self-assessment can help you see gaps and areas where your natural style can be strengthened into a resilient leadership style. Take a look at the following questions and statements, and rate yourself from 1 to 5 (1 = Never; 2 = Rarely; 3 = Sometimes; 4 = Often; 5 = Always).

Appearance. Do you look like a confident, competent leader? Rate yourself according to these criteria:

Good posture

Smooth gestures and movement

Neat, clean, appropriate attire

Good grooming

Eye Contact. Do you make steady eye contact with other people (without staring)?

Smile. Do you smile easily and naturally around people?

Vocal Confidence. Do you speak up clearly and confidently?

Friendliness. Do you treat people in a friendly, accepting way?

Precision. Are you precise but relaxed when speaking?

Enthusiasm. Are you positive and enthusiastic, but not overbearing?

Attentive Listening. Do you listen attentively to others?

Smarts. Are you up-to-date on the latest concepts and technology?

Lack of Pretense. Do you show your expertise without showing off?

Genuine Concern. Do you show genuine concern for others?

Integrity. Do you demonstrate high levels of integrity and honesty?

Objectivity. Are you fair, impartial, and objective in tough situations?

Courtesy and Respect. Do you show respect for others?

Avoidance of Gossip. Do you abstain from gossip and innuendo?

Confidentiality. Do you keep the secrets that others share with you?

BUILDING POWER AND INFLUENCE

Influence and power are the energizing forces that get things going and get things done. They are the indispensable tools of leaders. First, leaders must use their power to energize other people into action. Different people need different amounts of energizing to get going and get things done. Some folks need just a few words. Others need more than that. In all cases, a leader's use of power must fit the situation. Second, a leader must use influence when the direct use of power is impossible or inappropriate. This is especially important when dealing with peers and partners.

Before focusing on practices to build power and influence, you need to arm yourself with cogent insights about your current relationship to power and influence. To that end, three self-assessments follow.

The first self-assessment focuses on your *potential for power and influence*, so do not assume that any of your answers are good or bad. For example, your title and position in the organization may bring a lot of power with it—it would get a high mark—but do not interpret that to mean that you should rely on your title and position to carry an inordinate amount of force in energizing your direct reports.

Assessment #1: Your Power Potential

Ask yourself, "How much do these sources contribute to my power and influence?" Rate each item on a scale of 1 to 3:

1 = Contributes Very Little to my power and influence

2 = Contributes Somewhat to my power and influence

3 = Contributes Very Much to my power and influence

Sources of Power

☐ **Position** . . . the formal authority of my position, office, or title

☐ **Delegated Authority** . . . the specific authority delegated to me

☐ **Formal Rewards** . . . the tangible rewards I can give (e.g., money, awards)

☐ **Informal Rewards** . . . intangibles I can give (e.g., praise, attention, trust)

☐ **Formal Punishment** . . . punishment I can impose (e.g., firing, demotion)

☐ **Informal Punishment** . . . things I can deny (e.g., access, credit, time off)

☐ **Resources** . . . resources I can share or deny (e.g., money, people, data)

☐ **Performance "Under Fire"** . . . how I handle tough times, crises, and risks

☐ **Reputation** . . . my record for getting things done

☐ **Expertise** . . . my knowledge base, skills, and abilities

☐ **Political Savvy** . . . my awareness of and skill in political settings

☐ **Experience** . . . my experience base

☐ **Seniority**...my tenure in the organization or career field

☐ **Personality** . . . my presence, self-confidence, image, and agreeability

☐ **Speaking Skills** . . . my ability to inform and persuade

☐ **Decisiveness** . . . my ability to make tough decisions

☐ **Willpower** . . . my persistence, stamina, and mental toughness

☐ **Access to Powerful People** . . . my contacts with the powerful

☐ **Network** . . . my allies and supporters

☐ **Character** . . . my integrity, honesty, ethics, and moral standing

The higher your cumulative score, the higher your power potential. Again, remember this is just an assessment of your potential. To be truly powerful, you must use your power and influence to energize people to get things done. If you don't use it, you lose it.

Assessment #2: Your Power Profile

This second assessment helps you determine your power and influence profile. As the first quiz highlighted, your power comes partly from your position, your achievements, your relationships, and your resources. But a more important factor is your willingness to go out and get the things you want.

How often do you exhibit these behaviors with people other than your subordinates? Using the following 5-point ranking system, how would you characterize your behavior?

5 = Always

4 = Often

3 = Sometimes

2 = Seldom

1 = Never

Behaviors

☐ Present a strong and persuasive argument for my point of view.

☐ Go right to the top and deal with decision makers to make things happen.

☐ Use data, facts, statistics, and the testimony of others to convince people.

☐ Gather allies, backers, and supporters who are themselves powerful people.

☐ Appeal to the needs, interests, and desires of people I'm trying to sway.

☐ Use my charm, personality, or character to influence people.

☐ Show persistence in trying to get my way.

☐ Work around roadblocks in my way.

☐ Use my network of contacts to get inside information, resources, and help.

☐ Surround myself with competent people, even those who are smarter than I am.

☐ Find the uncommitted people and win them to my side.

☐ Exaggerate, use emotion, or create situations in order to get attention.

☐ Deal with people on a personal, social basis, not just on a professional basis.

☐ Disprove or discredit all opposing points of view.

☐ Give guarantees, promises, and assurances if it will help me.

☐ Use trades, favors, and rewards to get what I want.

☐ Use pressure, warnings, and threats to get what I want.

☐ Let people know about my successes.

☐ Associate with winners and avoid losers.

Add up your scores. If you scored above 70, you are probably very adept at using the power tactics and influence strategies necessary to get your way.

Assessment #3: Group Leadership Qualities

The third assessment invites you to rate your actions in leading a group of people. Rate the series of statements using this 3-point system:

1 = Not at all like me

2 = Somewhat like me

3 = Exactly like me

Statements

☐ I am fully aware of my power and influence and their sources.

> Power and influence are a function of perception. If you feel powerless and lacking in influence, you are. If you don't use it, you will be powerless. If people think you're powerful and influential, you are.

☐ I use the power and influence that I have to get results.

> Power and influence are not passive; they are active. They must be put into action. They're not a fixed commodity. You can increase them or lose them.

☐ I use my power and influence in an ethical manner.

> Power itself is neither good nor bad. It's the way you use power that is good or bad, right or wrong, ethical or unethical. Just keep in mind what nineteenth-century historian Lord Acton once remarked in a letter: "Power tends to corrupt, and absolute power corrupts absolutely."

☐ I use my power and influence in a way that fits.

> Use them in a way that's appropriate to your style, the people you're dealing with, the situation, and your organization's goals and norms.

☐ I draw on many sources of power and influence.

> The more sources you draw on to achieve results, the better. If you draw on several sources, produce results, and achieve success, others will want to follow you.

☐ I empower others.

> The more you wisely empower others, the more power you accumulate. You gain power by sharing it.

☐ I am aware of the limitations on my use of power and influence.

> Your use of power is subject to the will and whim of others; namely, your direct reports. You may state your intentions and give directions, but many critical choices are made by the people who are below you in the chain of command. If you believe you are in control, it is more a wish than a reality.

☐ I am aware of the traps involving the use of power and influence.

> Those traps include using more power than is necessary; squandering it on low-payoff pursuits; using it for the wrong reasons; and losing one's power and influence by not using them.

Influence

Now it's time to delve more into the mechanics of influence. When you want other people to do something for you but those people do not report to you directly or are not in positions that put them below you in the formal structure of the organization, then you need to exercise influence, not power. Here are thoughts on how to do that.

1. *Establish your goals, currencies, and strategy before trying to present your ideas.* Determine your goals—exactly what you want to achieve. Establish what you want the other person to know, accept, feel, and do. In addition, identify your currencies; that is, what you can give in exchange that others might want. You might be able to offer resources such as people, money, supplies, equipment, or facilities, as well as information or simple intangible rewards like goodwill, respect, supportiveness, and understanding. Also, know your going-in strategy. Are you prepared to take a hard or soft stance, an open or closed approach?

2. *As you begin to speak with the people you want to influence, probe first for more information.* Avoid launching right into a discussion of what you want. Take it slow and easy; use probing questions to determine what they need, want, or expect. As they respond, listen carefully to assess their readiness, willingness, and ability to understand or accept your request, recommendation, or proposal. And do something that is essential to building rapport: Find common ground. Discuss shared experiences.

3. *Present your request persuasively, but only after you let others speak.* Show how your request, recommendation, or proposal has unique strengths and advantages, and how it can benefit them. Use positive, rather than negative, associations and comparisons and weave in facts, statistics, evidence, and illustrations to prove your point. Appeal to people's sense of reason and goodwill, or to their emotions or curiosity.

4. *After making your presentation, get commitment for what you want.* Remain firm and assertive, but avoid power plays as you explain what you want other people to accept, believe, do, or feel. Ask them directly for approval, acceptance, belief, or action. Link the value and positive outcomes of their decision to the costs.

The more you can use stories, examples, and comparisons to help other people visualize the success associated with your ideas or request, the more they will get excited about your proposal.

The head of a major European subsidiary of a leading American toy company had a big problem. The company had been losing money for years. The company sold games and puzzles, but lacked a new product that could create buzz. Someone sent the CEO a funny-looking plastic extrusion with a happy face and multicolored stubbly hair. The CEO instinctively loved it. The sales director and nearly every other senior director of the company nearly laughed him out of the room when he advocated producing it. The CEO made the decision to launch the product, despite the overwhelming conclusion that it would be an unmitigated disaster.

Then the CEO devised a storytelling strategy, which served him well in two ways: It helped him launch the product successfully and get the company excited about the project.

He engaged a creative team in developing a backstory for the ugly dolls. They lived in a forest, where they sang songs and danced all day. Each doll had a playful name, loved life, and wanted nothing more than to be in the company of a happy little girl.

Many of those happy little girls went wild over the prototypes. They immediately cuddled the oddly shaped and oddly colored "monsters." The senior staff now had proof that the CEO was right, and when they needed to energize their skeptical employees about the new toy, all they had to do was tell the story of how much the children loved the dolls.

Sales quickly ran in the multimillions.

ENLIGHTENED OFFICE POLITICS

What does "politics" have to do with leadership? Isn't it better to play things straight and avoid the uncomfortable and messy entanglements associated with organizational politics?

Sometimes, to get results and protect the interests of their followers, leaders must engage effectively in organizational politics. In the opening of their book *Enlightened Office Politics* (AMACOM), Michael S. Dobson and Deborah S. Dobson assert, "Office politics is inevitable in every organization with three or more people in it. And you know you're faced with a choice: influencer or influenced, knowing or guessing, controller or controlled."

Over the last fifty years, most organizations have shifted from a top-down management paradigm to empowerment. Senior management has relinquished its power to control workloads and micromanage projects that could easily be handled by those with less authority. New leaders have more power than before. And more leadership is needed than ever before.

This shift is reflected in the language used at work. The use of "manager" as a title has fallen into disrepute in many organizations, with the new nomenclature including such terms as team leader and project coordinator. Power and responsibility are being delegated at all levels. In this case, when it comes to politics, it is no longer a matter of pleasing the boss; it is a matter of building your own constituency. You build your success by exercising your power in your organization's political arena.

Politics can be good and bad. How you participate in office politics is up to you, but there are a number of good reasons why you must. As a leader, you have not only goals and objectives, but also specific responsibilities to fulfill, including responsibilities that lie outside your own personal interests. For example:

→ *Achieving the Organization's Mission* (managing your resources and human resources to achieve the organizational mission and objectives)

→ *Procuring Needed Resources* (making sure your team has the resources it needs to achieve those objectives)

→ *Protecting Your Constituents* (doing all you personally can to ensure your group's success, and guarding against failure)

→ *Rewarding Your Constituents* (ensuring their efforts are justly rewarded)

→ *Ensuring Goodwill and Respect* (making your group's achievements known so that your employees get the recognition and benefits they deserve)

And since you have to participate in politics to fulfill your mission, the next question is, "How do you survive the process?"

Leaders must be prepared to protect their turf and the legitimate needs, interests, and resources of their team, their organization, and their position. The following checklists provide an overview of the practices that churn the political waters at work; as a corollary, they serve as a reminder of what types of actions you need to avoid.

Devious Political Tactics

- [ ] Making false promises or not delivering on promises
- [ ] Taking credit that is not deserved
- [ ] Discrediting the ideas, efforts, or accomplishments of others
- [ ] Creating traps or roadblocks to the efforts of others
- [ ] Denying the legitimate needs and requests of others
- [ ] Using stall tactics to make others waste their time and efforts
- [ ] Letting others dangle in the wind or struggle when in trouble
- [ ] Withholding, covering up, or delaying needed information
- [ ] Giving advice that is meant only to serve the leader's own interests
- [ ] Giving hollow or pretended support to others
- [ ] Subtly cutting others out of events, meetings, decisions, or plans
- [ ] Setting others up to fail or look bad

The Big Political Blunders

- [ ] Surprising the boss with bad news or hiding bad news
- [ ] Making an end run around the boss
- [ ] Being disloyal to the boss

☐ Complaining about the boss or upper management

☐ Being overly enthusiastic or demanding

☐ Not protecting things said confidentially

☐ Whining, complaining, criticizing

☐ Turning down an offer from the boss or upper management

☐ Challenging the boss's strongly held beliefs

☐ Burning bridges

In avoiding those devious behaviors or blunders and watching for them around every corner, take these *positive steps:*

➡ Create partnerships with powerful people.

➡ Defend your rights, interests, needs, and resources assertively.

➡ Negotiate, compromise, or even withdraw when appropriate.

In the last chapter of *Enlightened Office Politics*, Michael and Deborah Dobson offer forty rules to help you succeed in the game of office politics. They caution that the rules sometimes have to be broken, but only if there's a compelling reason to do so. Their rules are designed "to focus your thinking, to give you a model to analyze your current situation, to figure out some options for a dilemma." In summary, the rules are as follows:

1. *Deal with the way things are, not the way you think they ought to be or want them to be.* Start your political strategy process by writing down why things are the way they are, who benefits, and what factors stand in the way of change. Then, and only then, start making plans for change.

AMA Business Boot Camp

2. *Put yourself in the other person's shoes.* Try to look at every situation from the point of view of the others who are involved. Ideally, you will have three points of view working for you to help you grasp the politics of a situation: yours, the other person's, and the "fly on the wall" third party.

3. *Understand the underlying game of politics.* Always remember, if you want to lead and get things done, you will do so only through the instrument of politics.

4. *Establish your principles and ethics and always live by them, even when short-term advantages suggest otherwise.* Your principles can be one of your most effective political tools.

5. *Live your principles and life, not anyone else's, but give respect to the official party line.* Your principles and character have to come from within, and you can't be expected to absorb the official party line on every level. In fact, sometimes the party line is a myth, like when a company claims "Our product is the best." You have to say these words and then work around them to get a more realistic assessment; but if you reject the assumptions, the result will be that no one will listen to you.

6. *Deliberately acquire power and influence.* Make sure that your mental attitude about the acquisition of power is positive. Know why you want the power and then use it effectively.

7. *Know your reasons for being in the political arena—and know others' reasons, too.* When you know the reasons why other people are also deliberately seeking power and influence, you'll have valuable insight into their actions.

8. *Be a goal setter.* Goals make you more powerful and more effective, regardless of what you want to pursue. Review your goals on a regular basis. Make plans and strategies for achieving them.

9. *Develop your own intelligence network.* A necessary political skill is knowing how to do your own intelligence work. You need people who can and will tell you what's going on—people who know how to listen and can conduct research well.

10. *Work toward win-win solutions.* You almost always have to live with people after the political battle is over, so aim for a resolution that addresses the other person's wants and needs whenever possible.

11. *Discover the hidden keys to the executive suite.* Part of reading your own corporate culture is figuring out what the people who become senior executives have in common and what got them where they are. The answers generally fall into three categories: technical/job-related skills, interpersonal skills, and the old-boys (or old-girls) club. If you can't possibly succeed in all three, then cultivate and leverage the one(s) you can succeed in. After that, if you still get nowhere in terms of increased power and influence, leave that environment.

12. *Take a stand.* The purpose and value of being political is to get something done, and if you don't take a stand—even at some personal risk—then there is no point to being political in the first place.

13. *Know who your allies, opponents, fellow travelers, enemies, and neutrals are.* Also know why your supporters support you and why your opponents oppose you.

14. *Work to improve relationships and common interests.* While it may not be possible to avoid having any enemies, work to reduce their number by building relationships and trust, no matter what your political goal.

15. *Remember your friends ... and your enemies.* It's important for people to see there is benefit in being your friend, and that benefit is not provided to your enemy.

16. *Do favors for others and accept favors from others.* Build up the credits you have with others by going out of your way to help them. This allows you to ask for favors later when you need them.

17. *Be honest, or be quiet.* Your word must be your bond or your "career" as an office politician will be short-lived. Silence is often the best policy. It isn't dishonest unless you're deliberately withholding something that another person needs to know and has a right to know.

18. *If you don't have a stake in it, stay out of it.* Pick your fights carefully, and don't get involved if there's nothing at stake for you. Here's an exception: When you have all the facts and see that an injustice is clearly being done, your principles may win out over this rule.

19. *Look out for the "What's in it for me?" situation.* When you want to influence someone else's behavior, there is no more valuable insight than knowing what that individual's driving need or want is.

20. *Understand and respect the power of other people.* Consider the nature of other people's power—just as you have earlier been encouraged to consider the nature of your own power. Ask these questions in dealing with other people in power:

- Is the power a part of the person, or part of the position or situation?

- Is the power permanent or temporary?

- Does the person know how much power she possesses—or how to exploit it?

- What is the goal behind the power?

21. *Start with the relationship that exists and build from there.* If you want to improve a relationship with another person, you need to reflect first on why you do not already have a better relationship with the person—and there is always a reason.

22. *Avoid the double-cross.* A person who double-crosses cannot be trusted, and if you cannot be trusted, you will find it hard to be effective.

23. *Never make an enemy by accident.* You may discover you have offended someone without meaning to do so. When in doubt, ask. When an apology is in order, give it. Use the knowledge to increase your sensitivity in the future.

24. *Never attribute to malice what can be explained by stupidity.* When in doubt about the driver behind an insensitive action or remark, probe in an open-minded manner. You may well get an apology, and the upper hand, regardless of the reason.

25. *Respect those who oppose you.* Assuming your opponent has no business holding the power or influence in play is often self-destructive. Err in favor of overestimating the competition. It's safer.

26. *Deal firmly and quickly—and proportionally—with threats.* Remember the military definition of threat: the capability of someone to do you harm. Be aware of the threats to your goals and position and take prompt action. But keep this in mind: Sometimes just alerting the person that you are aware of what he has done to threaten you is enough to make the person back down.

27. *Put the squeeze on when necessary.* Earn a reputation for being supportive and helpful so that when you need help, you can ask for it clearly and assertively—and get it.

28. *Bend with the prevailing wind.* This advice is not a matter of running contrary to your principles, but rather managing the reality that you cannot force people in a direction they don't want to go. Bend a little, but keep heading in your intended direction and with time, using your influence, others will follow your lead.

29. *Examine job assignments for hidden traps.* When you say yes to a project, you aren't merely agreeing to do what has been articulated, you are also agreeing to the hidden assumptions of your customers, boss, or colleagues. Ask questions before saying "yes," and try to ferret out the hidden agendas, the possible need for resources not readily available, and the benefits to key players of the project's outcome, among other key factors.

30. *Study the political environment, looking for factors that will affect how other people will act.* Center on the objectives that set people on a particular path in the first place. Their desire to achieve those objectives shapes their behavior.

31. *Learn how to manage change.* Remember that your credibility and power to make changes must be earned. Use effective communication and be clear about the benefits to your customers or direct reports about making the change.

32. *Know the organization's internal image and how it relates to the real world.* One disadvantage of propaganda is that the person who generates it often ends up believing it. Effective politicians work very hard not to believe their own propaganda. Make a habit of never overestimating your competition and of generating truthful statements you can tell yourself about the realities of your contributions and accomplishments.

33. *Respect the chain of command.* The chain of command is one of the factors that gives you a certain amount of power; respecting that it gives people senior to you relatively more contributes to their acknowledgment of the power you legitimately hold.

34. *Promote your accomplishments.* Do not assume that others pay attention to the great things you do. Write a report after you score a success with a customer, for example. There's no need to be pushy, but make sure a record of your success enters the right file.

35. *Protect your reputation.* Your reputation is your primary political asset, so defend it. There are two potential sources of damage to your reputation: other people and yourself. Watch yourself and be sure that you deserve a good reputation; then, when someone else takes a swing at it, public opinion will more likely be on your side.

36. *Learn something new.* Part of your political strategy should be to develop yourself into an even greater asset than you already are. Political skills may get you promoted, but knowledge will make it obvious you deserve the promotion.

37. *Keep your word, both positively and negatively.* Parents know this rule well in disciplining children. If you promise dessert after the kid eats his peas, you'd better deliver dessert when he follows through. The opposite applies.

38. *Go to lunch with different people.* Lunch isn't about food; it's about relationships. Use the time and experience to broaden your network of contacts.

39. *Think several steps ahead.* The process goes like this: First, stop and think. Second, consider the other person's goals and strategies. Third, roll the possibilities for your action around in your head to see if you find anything wrong with them.

40. *Take time to plan.* You don't plan because you expect reality to conform to your plan. You plan because the act of planning helps you to be better prepared for the unforeseen.

MOTIVATING DIFFICULT PEOPLE

The bottom line on leadership is getting people to do what you want them to do. What motivates them? What energizes them? What inspires them to line up their arrows in the same direction as yours?

People who already share your point of view and consider the goals and strategies you have articulated as their own only need a plan and course of action to follow your lead. Then there are the difficult people, those who see the flaw in any plan except their own, don't think the course of action lets them "show off" enough, or want to knock you down in public—among other horrors facing a leader.

Consider some types of difficult people you may know, as described in these scenarios.

The Staller

Joe Brown holds up everybody and everything. You are trying to lead your group to completion of a major project, but Joe keeps asking you to delay the deadline. The group has nicknamed Joe "the Staller."

The Emotional Hothead

Lois Green is a member of your group and she is typically a good performer. The problem with Lois is that she blows up at you and other team members when things don't go her way. When you ask Lois for a status update on a major client project, she storms out of your office.

The Complainer

Ivan White complains about everything. He doesn't like the layout of the office space, he complains about the way his coworkers design programs, and he has just complained about the way you handled a department meeting.

The Backstabber

Nora Black, your fellow sales manager, is very friendly and helpful when you are together. You recently voiced some concerns to Nora privately about your group's customer service skills, without mentioning names. You have just heard that Nora has been complaining to your boss about your management style and your direct reports' lack of customer service skills. Apparently it's not the first time she has complained about you.

Ms. or Mr. Perfect

Peter Kelly thinks he knows it all. Whenever you try to offer tips on how to utilize more effective e-solutions, Peter claims he knows best. He is very bright, keeps up-to-date in this field, and is a good performer. However, many field experts have told you that your group needs to change technologies, and in Peter's perfect world, the current technology is the best.

The common challenge in each of these scenarios is understanding enough about other people's motivation to turn them into supportive and contributing members of the team. Specifically, you have to do the following:

- *Determine why the Staller resists moving forward.* Start by looking at his participation in other projects in which he contributed to progress. Why there and not here? If Joe always stalls, then Joe might need a different work environment. Figure out to what extent his talents and career goals match his job.
- *Help the Emotional Hothead sort real stress from day-to-day demands.* As a corollary, help her respond to stress a different way. Lois explodes when in a mild state of "fight or flight," that is, when she feels threatened. Take her aside and let her know that ongoing requests for information have no value judgments associ-

ated with them. It might also help to let her know that other people get stressed out when she explodes, and that hurts the entire team.

➜ *Turn the Complainer from a problem seeker to a problem solver.* Show complainers like Ivan how problem seeking is a valuable skill—when it's applied right. It's a good thing that someone has the keen eye to notice that some situations and practices don't meet high standards. The observation is appreciated by others when it a) shows a sense of priorities related to the project at hand and b) is followed by a suggestion on correcting the problem.

➜ *Match the approach to Backstabbers with their personal style.* Some backstabbers default to a passive-aggressive style of retaliation if they feel the least bit threatened by a person or by information. Direct confrontation will only aggravate the situation, so ask questions that invite information about the person's goals and desires. Other backstabbers use the tactic consciously to reduce someone else's power. With someone like that, be direct. Find out what Nora wants and how you can provide benefit to each other.

➜ *Get Ms. or Mr. Perfect to take ownership of the proposal and its success.* If Peter thinks the proposal could not have come about without his insights, or could not be implemented effectively without his skills, he will be more inclined to reduce his resistance to the idea.

When it comes to difficult people, we only see their external behaviors: their words, their actions, and their body language. For most people, however, the real source of their lack of motivation or difficult behavior is internal and is the result of things we cannot easily see, like the person's:

→ Self-image

→ Values

→ Desires

→ Attitudes

→ Needs

→ Beliefs

→ Experiences

→ Interpretations

In some instances, though, the catalyst for difficult behavior is external. Sometimes our own behavior provokes the other person or enables bad behavior to continue. It could be a personality clash, our leadership style, or the way in which we communicate. The only way to know for sure is to move beyond the behavior and connect with the person one-on-one. You must maintain a careful balance between finding out enough about other people to resolve your difficulties with them and becoming an amateur psychologist.

Let's use these tips on dealing with difficult people in particular scenarios to set the stage for defining a process for dealing with difficult people in general. Here is a seven-step process to guide you. When confronted by a difficult person, use this process to control your emotions, manage the other person's emotions, and start to solve the problem.

1. **Absorb** what the difficult person is saying. Get the person's point of view. Watch and listen without reacting, then look within to your true feelings.

   Ask yourself: Why does this behavior seem difficult to me? Is there another perspective? What does my reaction say about me?

2. **Avoid** getting emotionally involved. If extremely provoked, say:

    "Let's not get in an argument over this and destroy our relationship. Can we set this aside until we can approach this issue calmly?"

3. **Ask** for clarification and more information. Keep the person talking.

    Use phrases such as, *"Tell me more." "What do you mean by that?" "What more can you tell me?"*

4. **Acknowledge** what the person has said. Restate what you have heard. Describe what you heard the person say and what that individual is feeling.

    "So what I am hearing you say is that . . . and it seems that you feel . . . "

5. **Ask** the person to suggest how the problem could be solved.

    "What do you think should be done to resolve this problem?"

6. **Agree** with something the other person has said.

    "I agree with you that ..."

7. **Add** your point of view, only after you understand the person's perspective on the problem and proposed solution. (Avoid starting with *but*, which is confrontational, rather than an effort to supplement the information presented.)

    "Let me add my point of view now. I strongly feel that ..."

General guidance for dealing with difficult people includes these tips:

➜   *Identify the real reasons for the difficult behavior.* Difficult behavior is often just a symptom of a deeper unresolved problem.

➜   *Work together to fix the problem.* Don't just try to fix the behavior.

- *Visualize a positive outcome for a change in the behavior.* Remember that your goal is to promote positive behavior.
- *Be firm and consistent, and remember your long-range goals.* Don't let yourself get stuck in a rut dealing with difficult people.

As a final note on motivating people in your role as leader, consider your network of influence. As important as knowing *how* to influence is knowing *whom* to influence. Which people are your best allies in implementing the changes needed to get more engagement and commitment from your direct reports? Who in your network of contacts can help you achieve your objectives? It helps to map your network and identify those people who are in positions to help you initiate and implement change.

The map is a useful tool in identifying the people you can influence—and the people you know that can influence others. Your efforts to motivate others can have a ripple effect through them.

It all starts with you.

SECTION II ACTION ITEMS

To begin cultivating senior management skills, you need to climb a ladder or even a mountain at least in a figurative sense. The point is that your view of challenges, including tense interactions among your direct reports, must be broader than the one you had before you joined the ranks of management.

❑ *Develop a strategic frame of reference.* It will guide you through the maze of options that can occur with different problems. It will help you get an organized sense of goals, tasks, roles, relationships, and what constitutes progress.

❑ *Practice using a SWOT analysis.* It will focus your team on the areas where you are collectively strong and the areas that need work, as well as what factors and situations may currently, or in the future, lead to opportunities or problems.

❑ *Make sure your team understands that you need an honest ranking of what needs to be fixed to meet the expectations of your stakeholders.* By the same token, lead them in being forthright in admitting "we're doing too much of this, and not enough of that." That's not cause for punishment; it's cause for correction.

❑ *Conduct a self-assessment.* Part of strengthening your leadership abilities involves knowing your natural leadership style. Standardized tools such as the MBTI can help you to gain insights about your tendencies and then build on that knowledge. Self-assessment regarding how senior management and your direct reports see you, and why they see you that way, will also give you a baseline on your leadership characteristics. One caution: Don't let test results box you in. They

SECTION II ACTION ITEMS

provide insights, but are not absolute predictors of how you can develop.

❏ *Communicate clearly, with facts and inspiration.* Tell your direct reports not only what's going on, but also help them understand why they should feel motivated to perform at their peak.

❏ *Stay alert to generational differences among your direct reports.* Their values, perception of workplace priorities, and behavior can differ markedly. Nonetheless, it's your job to cultivate enough common focus that everyone wants to move in the same direction.

❏ *Leverage your leadership style by tweaking it, as necessary, for your various audiences.* You don't want to appear to be different people; rather, you want different people to relate to your leadership appropriately and notice how consistent you are as a leader.

❏ *Use body language to your advantage.* Both movements and vocal characteristics send signals about your level of confidence, interest in other people and openness to their ideas, energy for the task at hand, and even your integrity.

❏ *Keep the rules of enlightened office politics handy.* It is rare, indeed, for an office to have such interpersonal harmony that conflicts and tension never arise.

❏ *Always remember that part of leadership involves motivation.* Just as everyone in your workplace doesn't want to eat the same

Cont'd.

SECTION II ACTION ITEMS

thing for lunch, neither do they want the same speech or same perk as a route to motivation. Never just dismiss employees who appear to stall all the time or complain regularly. They may have an odd way of showing it, but it's possible that's their way of saying, "I want to contribute so much more."

❑ *Be mindful of your network of influence.* Know your allies—that is, the people who can help you effect changes in the workplace, implement plans, and raise the level of commitment among your employees. Their actions can have the ripple effect you desire through the organization. It all starts with you and it all loops back to one of the first lessons in the book: Being a manager is about getting work done through other people.

Appendix A

SELF-ASSESSMENT ON COMFORT LEVEL
WITH DELEGATION

As mentioned in Chapter 2, this self-assessment gives you a sense of your comfort level with delegating. The more often you can check the "always" box for each question, the better your skills at delegating.

When I am overloaded with work, I look to my direct reports to take on some of my work.

    ❐ always ❐ usually ❐ sometimes ❐ never

I let my direct reports know what I expect of them.

    ❐ always ❐ usually ❐ sometimes ❐ never

After I have delegated a project, all of my team members know who is leading the project and his/her level of authority on the project.

    ❐ always ❐ usually ❐ sometimes ❐ never

When I delegate work to any of my direct reports, I provide them with all of the information I have on the subject.

    ❐ always ❐ usually ❐ sometimes ❐ never

In my organization, delegation is perceived as an opportunity for growth and recognition.

◻ always   ◻ usually   ◻ sometimes   ◻ never

I consider the skills and knowledge of my direct reports before assigning them a project.

◻ always   ◻ usually   ◻ sometimes   ◻ never

I stress the results I am looking for, not how to achieve them, when I assign work to my direct reports.

◻ always   ◻ usually   ◻ sometimes   ◻ never

It is easy for me to delegate work to qualified employees.

◻ always   ◻ usually   ◻ sometimes   ◻ never

After delegating work, I stay in touch with my direct report on the progress being made.

◻ always   ◻ usually   ◻ sometimes   ◻ never

I hold the assigned direct report responsible for the results of the work.

◻ always   ◻ usually   ◻ sometimes   ◻ never

Appendix B

Coaching Planning Worksheet

Use this tool in preparation for coaching sessions with your direct reports. Take the time to answer each of the questions before you start your meeting. This six-step exercise will help you stay on target and not be sidetracked by the other person. This focus enables you to maintain a professional position when you are feeling uncomfortable.

Coaching Planning Worksheet

EMPLOYEE NAME _____

MEETING DATE _____

DEVELOPMENTAL LEVEL FOR THIS TASK/SITUATION _____

Step 1: *Set the Stage.* Describe in detail why this meeting is being held.

Step 2: *Formulate and Focus the Issue.* What approach will you suggest to improve or enhance the performance in this situation?

Cont'd.

Coaching Planning Worksheet

Step 3: *Get Agreement.* How will you get agreement from your direct report that this coaching action will be beneficial for him/her?

Step 4: *Generate Possible Solutions and/or Alternatives.* How will you encourage your direct report to brainstorm with you?

Step 5: *Set Goals and Develop an Action Plan.* With your direct report, set specific plans that include actions, timelines, and consequences, if appropriate.

Step 6: *Monitor (Next Steps).* What is your plan to follow up?

Appendix C

Project Management Planning Template

GENERIC PROJECT SCOPE STATEMENT

Project Name: _____   Project Number: _____

Project Manager: _____   Date: _____

A. BUSINESS JUSTIFICATION
(TAKEN FROM THE PROJECT CHARTER)

Business Need/Opportunity: _____

Product Description (Solution): _____

Deliverables: _____

B. PROJECT DESCRIPTION

Project Boundaries (Inclusions/Exclusions): _____

Completion Criteria: _____

Risk Management: _____

Project Constraints: _____

Impacts/Cross-Impacts: _____

Measures of Project Success: _____

Milestones: _____

Project Requirements/Specifications: _____

Assumptions: _____

Product Acceptance Criteria: _____

Budget Limitations: _____

C. ROLES AND PROJECT STAKEHOLDERS

ROLES:

Project Sponsor	
Client/Customer	
Project Manager	
Project Coordinator	
Core Project Team Members	
Subject Matter Experts	

STAKEHOLDERS:

Area/Organization	Name	Title	Role

D. PROJECT METHODOLOGY

Planned Approach: _____

Configuration/Change Management: _____ _____

Approval Requirements: _____

E. ESTIMATES

SCHEDULE:

Project Milestones	Target Date

RESOURCE REQUIREMENTS–TEAM AND SUPPORT RESOURCES:

Project Milestones	Quantity

TOTAL PERSONNEL RESOURCES: _____

COSTS *(INITIAL):*

Labor	
Internal IT	$
Internal Business	$
External	$
Hardware	$
Software	$
Materials	$
Equipment	$
Facilities	$
Supplies	$
Other	$

TOTAL $: _____

FUNDING SCHEDULE: _____

F. APPROVALS

Scope statement will be approved by:

Project Manager: _____   *Functional Manager:* _____

Project Sponsor: _____   *Functional Manager:* _____

Customer/Client: _____   *Other key stakeholders, as required:*

Functional Manager: _____   _____

Functional Manager: _____

Name	Title/Position	Signature	Date

Glossary

Active Listening Demonstrating with your body language and your choice of questions and comments that you are fully engaged in the conversation.

Closed-Ended Questions One of four major types of questioning styles. (See also Open-ended, Probing, and Hypothetical.) Closed-ended questions solicit a "yes" or "no" answer rather than a narrative response.

Competency A skill, trait, quality, or characteristic that contributes to a person's ability to effectively perform the duties and responsibilities of a job.

Critical Path Path made up of activities that have zero float. (See also Float.) Activities must start on time and finish on time for the project to be completed on time.

Critical Path Method (CPM) Most common technique for building a project schedule; supported by most project management software.

Duration Estimates In project management, the amount of time the task is expected to take on a calendar, from the time the task is started until it is completed.

Effort Estimates In project management, the amount of actual labor required to perform the task.

Flat Organization Organizational structure in which positions in middle management are reduced or eliminated to bring upper management in direct contact with the rest of the staff.

Float The amount of time that a deliverable can be delayed without causing a delay to other work packages (free float) or the project completion date (total float).

Functional Manager In project management, the manager of a functional or administrative area of the business who provides resources or expertise; the functional manager may be a specialist such as a programmer or designer.

Gantt Chart A type of bar chart designed to illustrate a project schedule.

Gate Review Board In project management, a formal group of senior executives convened to evaluate the status of a project and determine whether it should proceed through the next "gate."

Herzberg's Model A system for workplace motivation centered on Frederick Herzberg's motivator-hygiene theory.

Hygiene Factors (also known as Maintenance Factors) In motivation discussions, those factors pinpointed by Frederick Herzberg that prevent dissatisfaction; namely, pay, status, security, working conditions, fringe benefits, and policies and administrative practices.

Hypothetical Questions One of four major types of questioning styles. (See also Closed-ended, Open-ended, and Probing.) Hypothetical questions invite speculation.

Importance/Performance (I/P) Matrix A tool for evaluating your competitive strengths and weaknesses through your customers' eyes.

MBWA Acronym for management by walking around.

Motivational Factors In motivation discussions, those factors pinpointed by Frederick Herzberg that engender satisfaction; namely, achievement, responsibility, meaningfulness, recognition, and opportunities for growth and advancement.

Myers-Briggs Type Indicator (MBTI) A standardized personality test sometimes used to determine a natural match between an individual and a career or task.

Nonexempt Worker A worker who is entitled by law to receive overtime pay.

Open-Ended Questions One of four major types of questioning styles. (See also Closed-ended, Probing, and Hypothetical.) Open-ended questions encourage people to talk.

PAL Formula Acronym for purpose, agenda, and length, which are the core concepts in planning a good meeting.

Parking Lot Items Discussion topics introduced in a meeting that are not germane to the meeting but are nonetheless worth addressing in another context.

PMBOK Guide A document produced by the Project Management Institute (PMI)—officially titled *A Guide to the Project Management Body of Knowledge*—containing current standards for project management. The references in this book are to the fourth edition of the guide.

Probing Questions One of four major types of questioning styles. (See also Closed-ended, Open-ended, and Hypothetical.) Probing questions poke for explanations ("why" or "how"), clarification, or honesty.

Product Scope In project management, "the features and functions to be included in a product, service, or result" (definition from the *PMBOK Guide*).

Project Management Professional (PMP) A credential earned through the Project Management Institute that reflects thorough knowledge of the *PMBOK Guide* as well as hands-on project management experience.

Project Manager (PM) Person responsible for achieving project objectives.

Project Scope In project management, "the work that must be done in order to deliver a product, service, or result, with the specified features and functions" (from the *PMBOK Guide*).

Requirement In project management, "a condition or capability that must be met or possessed by a system, product, result, or component to satisfy a contract, standard, specification, or other formally imposed document" (from the *PMBOK Guide*).

Responsibility Assignment Matrix (RAM) A common tool used to connect people with the work on the project.

Risk Register A table documenting risks associated with a project.

Scope In project management, "the sum of the products, services, and results to be provided as a project" (from the *PMBOK Guide*).

Scope Creep In project management, the expansion of project scope without going through a formal process of change control.

SITREP Acronym for situation report, a very brief status update directed at a decision maker.

SMART (Employee Performance Objectives) Acronym for specific, measurable, attainable, relevant, trackable and time-bound. SMART is a framework or model for developing performance objectives for direct reports.

SMART (Project Management Requirements) Acronym for specific, measurable, agreed-to, realistic, and time-bound.

SME Acronym for subject matter expert; often seen in descriptions of members of a project team.

SPARK Acronym to describe the behavior of leadership; that is, share information, play to strengths, ask for input/appreciate different ideas, recognize/respond to individual needs, and keep your commitments.

Sponsor In project management, the source of financial resources. The sponsor may also be the project champion or the person who serves as an interface between the project and senior management.

Stakeholder In project management, people with different levels of responsibility for a project, authority over it, and level of interest or activity. Stakeholders may include customers/end-users, the project sponsor (funding source), the project manager, project team, functional managers, vendors, and others with a vested interest in the success of the project.

Strategic Frame of Reference A dynamic planning and implementation tool used in developing a strategic approach to addressing problems and challenges.

SWOT Acronym for identifying your work group's specific strengths, weaknesses, opportunities, and threats.

Triple Constraints In project management, the factors of time, cost, and scope requirements; they are often depicted in the form of a triangle, suggesting interdependence of factors that frame a project.

WBS Dictionary (See also Work Breakdown Structure.) A document containing detailed information about the various elements in the WBS; it is viewed as a useful resource by project managers, team members, and other stakeholders for establishing common understandings of milestones and performance measurements.

Work Breakdown Structure (WBS) An outline of the work needed to meet project objectives; that is, all of the work that needs to be done on the project—project work and product work.

Work Package (WP) Smaller element of the WBS. Work packages help to organize large, complex projects.

Index

AMA Handbooks from AMACOM

The Book Publishing Division of American Management Association

AMACOM
Publishing division of
AMERICAN MANAGEMENT ASSOCIATION
AMA

The AMA Handbook of Project Management
Third Edition
9780814415429   Hardcover $79.95

The AMA Handbook of Leadership
9780814415139   Hardcover $29.95

The AMA Handbook of Financial Risk Management
9780814417447   Hardcover $75.00

The AMA Handbook of Public Relations
9780814415252   Hardcover $35.00

The AMA Handbook of Business Documents: Guidelines and Sample Documents that Make Business Writing Easy
9780814417690   Paperback $19.95

The AMA Handbook of Business Letters
Fourth Edition
9780814420126   Hardcover $29.95

The AMA Handbook of Business Writing: The Ultimate Guide to Style, Grammar, Punctuation, Usage, Construction, and Formatting
9780814415894   Hardcover $34.95

The AMA Handbook of Due Diligence
9780814413821   Hardcover $295.00

Administrative Assistant's and Secretary's Handbook
Fourth Edition
9780814417607   Hardcover $34.95

Print edition details as noted above. Most AMACOM titles are also available as Ebooks. Please visit your favorite EBook supplier for pricing.